Instant
Immersion

French™

developed and written by Mary March, M.A.

TOPICS
ENTERTAINMENT®

TOPICS
ENTERTAINMENT®

© 2008 Topics Entertainment, Inc.

3401 Lind Ave. S.W. Renton, WA 98057 U.S.A.

www.InstantImmersion.com

Instant Immersion™

developed and written by Mary March, M.A.

Edited by Naty de Menezes
Illustrations by Elizabeth Haidle
Art Director: Paul Haidle
Design by Paul Haidle
Maps by Lonely Planet®

Printed on 100% recycled paper. Printed in the U.S.A.

TABLE OF CONTENTS

Bonus! Portable Video Phrase Book DVD

INTRODUCTION

Bienvenue (welcome) to *Instant Immersion French*™! An understanding of other cultures is critical in becoming part of a larger global community. Knowing how to communicate in other languages is one way to facilitate this process. You have chosen a truly global language to learn. There are diverse francophone (French-speaking) cultures in Europe, Canada, Africa, and the Caribbean, having a worldwide influence on cuisine, fashion, dance, theatre, architecture, and arts. French is also the official working language of many international organizations and is the second language used on the Internet.

Now let's get down to learning some French. Did you know that close to half of all English vocabulary has roots in the French language? This means you already know the meaning of many French words such as: *radio, courage, police, concert, train, possible,* and *restaurant.* Other French words look very much like their English equivalents: *musique, banane, nationalité, bicyclette, hôpital, ordinaire, and lettre.* You just have to learn the pronunciation. (And you will see that learning French pronunciation is not as difficult as you might think!)

This book will help you learn the basics of communicating in French in a way that will be fun and easy for you. We include many popular phrases and expressions and show you how these are used in real life through example conversations and stories. Our book also provides an easy pronunciation system that will give you the confidence you need to speak French. A wide range of interesting and valuable topics give you a firm grounding in the language, including how to order food like a local, how to travel comfortably within the country, even what to do when things go 'wrong'.

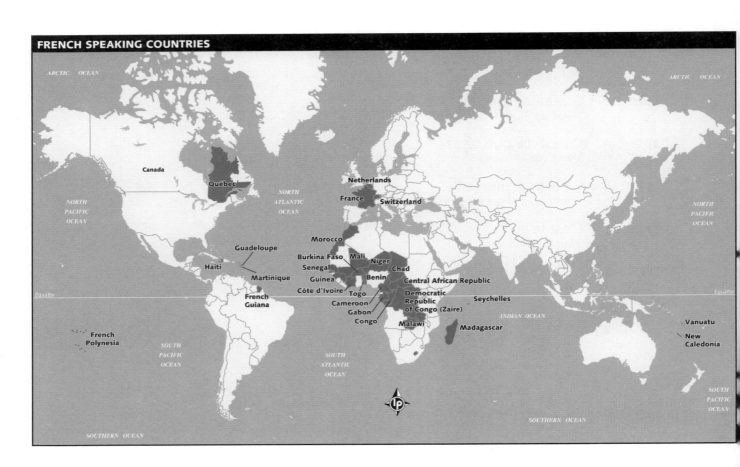

FRENCH SPEAKING COUNTRIES

PRONUNCIATION GUIDE

VOWELS

Paying particular attention to the four accent marks used on some of the vowels will help you learn the sounds that correspond with them. Yes, it does make a difference in which direction the accent mark points! Note: See chapter 2 for an explanation of nasal vowels.

French Letters	Symbol	English/French Examples
a, à, â	ah	ahh/papa *(pah-pah)*
é, er, ez	ay	day/bébé *(bay-bay)*
et	ay	et *(ay)*
ai	ay	j'ai *(zhay)*
ê, è	eh	pet/mère *(mehr)*
e + 2 consonants	eh	belle *(behl)*
et, ei, ai	eh	ballet *(bah-leh)*, seize *(sehz)*/mais *(meh)*
e,	uh	the/le *(luh)*/prenez *(pruh-nay)*
eu	uh	peu *(puh)*, jeune *(zhuhn)*
i, y,	ee	meet/midi *(mee-dee)*, Sylvie *(seel-vee)*
ill, ail, eil	y	yes/famille *(fah-mee-y)*, travail *(trah-vahy)*, soleil *(soh-lehy)*
ill	eel	eel/ville *(veel)*, village *(vee-lahzh)*,
o, ô, au, eau	o	boat/mot *(moh)*, hôtel *(o-tehl)*, aussi *(o-see)*, beau *(bo)*
o	oh	love/homme *(ohm)*, téléphone *(tay-lay-fohn)*
ou, où, oû	oo	youth/douze *(dooz)*, beaucoup *(bo-coo)*
oy, oi	wah	wash/moi *(mwah)*
u	ew*	tu *(tew)*, salut *(sah-lew)*

*This sound does not exist in English. It is not difficult to pronounce, but it does take some practice. Try this: Put your lips in the position of saying oo (as in "moo"), but say ee (as in "me").

CONSONANTS

Most French consonants sound like they do in English. Here are some of the consonants and corresponding symbols you will see in this book:

ch	sh	chocolat *(shoh-koh-lah)*, chaud *(sho)*
g (before e, i, y)	zh	(like the S in "measure"), âge *(ahzh)*,
gn	ny	(like the "n" in "onion"), montagne *(mohN-tah-nyuh)*
j	zh	(like the S in "measure"), Jacques *(zhahk)*

Important! Beware that most consonants at the end of a word are not pronounced. In the word "restaurant" (rehs-to-rahN), for example, the final "n" and "t" are not pronounced, and in plurals, the final "s" is not pronounced: hôtels (o-tehl). (Note also that "h" is always silent.) Only c, r, f, and l (the consonants in the word "careful") are usually pronounced at the end of words.

The French "r" will also need some practice to get it right. If you can gargle, then you can produce this sound. Try to say "Sara" making the "r" way back in your throat. Let your tongue rest on the bottom of your mouth when you say the French "r".

This book has 16 chapters. You can work through the book chapter by chapter or skip around to the topics that most interest you. Study the expressions and vocabulary before reading the dialog or story. Say them out loud to practice your pronunciation. Read through the dialog or story as many times as you need in order to understand it. Then read it out loud. Check your answers to the exercises in the Answer Key at the back of the book. Finally, get in a French mood! Put on a beret, drink French wine, put on an Edith Piaf tape, buy a baguette, speak English with a French accent, whatever it takes....
Amusez-vous bien! (Have fun!)

CHAPTER 1

(bohN-zhoor)
Bonjour!
Good morning!

Baseball. Parking. Titanic. Taxi. Madonna. Now say each of those words with the stress on the last syllable. *Voilà (vwah-LAH)*! You have a French accent. Putting a slight stress on the last syllable of words is a general rule in French that is good to keep in mind. Whenever you come across a French word with more than one syllable, just remember to put that stress on the final syllable.

You should also know that people who speak French like to link (or connect) their words. If you read this sentence "I ate an egg at eight" linking the words together, it would sound like this: *"I yay-ta-neg-ga-teight"*. This is what happens a lot in French when words begin with vowels and one reason why it is often difficult to pick out individual words when you hear the language. You will know when you need to connect the words as you read the pronunciation above the words in each chapter. The following expressions are examples of linking words together.

(sah meh tay-gahl)
Ça m'est égal.
It's all the same to me.

(ohN nyee-vah)
On y va!
Let's go!

VOCABULARY

(eel)
il
he

(unuhm)
un homme
man

(luh ma-taN)
le matin
morning

(el)
elle
she

(ewn fahm)
une femme
woman

(pahr-lay)
parler
to speak

(boN-zhoor)
Bonjour.
Good morning.

(sah vah)
Ça va?
How are you?

(sah vah beeyahN)
Ça va bien.
I'm fine.

(twa)
toi (familiar)
you

(vuh)
veux
want

(ah-lay)
aller
to go

(praNdr)
prendre
to take
*(but with food or
meals, it means
"to have")*

(mahN-zhay)
manger
to eat

(luh day-zhuh-nay)
le déjeuner
lunch

(luh deenay)
le dîner
dinner

(luh puh-tee day-zhuh-nay)
le petit déjeuner
breakfast

DIALOG

(seh luh ma-taN) (ewn fahm) (Leez) (ay unN nohm) (Pol) (pahrl)
C'est le matin. Une femme (Lise) et un homme (Paul) parlent.
it is   and   are speaking

(bohN-zhoor) (sah vah)
Lise: "Bonjour Paul. Ça va?"

(ay twa)
Paul: "Bonjour, Lise. Ça va bien. Et toi?"
and you?

(oo vuh tew praNdr luh puh-tee day-zhuh-nay)
Lise: "Ça va. Où veux–tu prendre le petit déjeuner?"
where do you want to have

(sa meh tay-gahl) (ohN puh ah-lay o kah-fay duh lo-tehl)
Paul: "Ça m'est égal. On peut aller au café de l'hôtel."
we can   to the   of the

(zhuh vuh mahN-zhay uhN krwa-sahN)
"Je veux manger un croissant."
I want to eat a crescent-shaped bread.

(mwa-ohsee) (ahlor, oh Nyee-vah)
Lise: "Moi aussi. Alors, On y va!"
me too   then

PRACTICE

le petit déjeuner	le dîner	veux	prendre
le déjeuner	où	tu	aller

Fill in the blanks using words from the box above.

1. Où __veux-tu__ prendre __le dîner__ ? *(8 pm)*

2. Où veux-tu __prendre le déjeuner__ ? *(12:00 noon)*

3. __Où__ veux-tu prendre __le petit déjeuner__ ? *(8 am)*

4. __Où__ veux-tu aller?

MATCHING

Match the sentence with the picture.

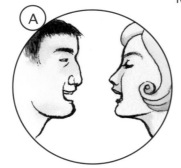

___E___ 1. Où veux-tu prendre le petit déjeuner?

___A___ 2. Une femme et un homme parlent.

___D___ 3. Je veux manger.

___B___ 4. C'est le matin.

___C___ 5. Ça m'est égal.

___F___ 6. Alors, on y va!

FOCUS

SUBJECT PRONOUNS

Singular			Plural		
je	*(zhuh)*	I	nous	*(noo)*	we
tu	*(tew)*	you (familiar)	vous	*(voo)*	you (familiar)
vous	*(voo)*	you (formal)	vous	*(voo)*	you (formal)
il	*(eel)*	he, it (m)	ils	*(eel)*	they (m)
elle	*(ehl)*	she, it (f)	elles	*(ehl)*	they (f)
on	*(ohN)*	one, we			

VERB FOCUS

(mahN-zhay)
manger
to eat

(zhuh mahN zhuN puh)
Je mange un peu.
I eat a little.

(noo mahN-zhoN bo-koo)
Nous mangeons beaucoup.
We eat a lot.

(tew mahNzh duh lah veeyaNd)
Tu manges de la viande.
You eat meat.
(singular/informal)

(voo mahN-zhay day paht)
Vous mangez des pâtes.
You eat pasta.
(plural and singular/informal)

(ehl mahNzh dahN lah vwa-tewr)
Elle mange dans la voiture.
She eats in the car.

(eel mahNzh sewr lah plahzh)
Elles mangent sur la plage.
They (female) eat on the beach.

(eel mahNzh sewr lah plahzh)
Il mange sur la plage.
He eats on the beach.

(eel mahNzh o lee)
Ils mangent au lit.
They (male) eat in bed.

NOTES

Tu or *vous?* The French use *tu* when talking to a relative, friend, child or animal. Teenagers use *tu* with each other even when they first meet. If a person older than you asks you to *tutoyer*, he/she is not asking you to dance, but is in fact giving you permission to use *tu* (informal) rather than *vous* (formal) when speaking to that person. In order to avoid being impolite, it's best to begin using *vous* with people when you first meet.

On means "one" in the sense of "people": *Ici on parle français.* (People speak French here.) Important: In spoken French, *on* is widely used instead of *nous. Nous parlons français = On parle français.* (We speak French.) Be careful to use the third person singular form of the verb.

(prahNdr)
PRENDRE
to take

je prends	*(zhuh prahN)*	*I take*
tu prends	*(tew prahN)*	*you take*
il, elle, on prend	*(eel, ehl, ohN prahN)*	*he, she one takes*
nous prenons	*(noo pruh-nohN)*	*we take*
vous prenez	*(voo pruh-nay)*	*you take*
ils, elles prennent	*(eel, ehl prehn)*	*they take*

Here are some common expressions with *prendre*:

(ohn vah prahNdr luh ~~pe-tee~~ day-zhuh-nay) [handwritten: puh-]
On va prendre le petit déjeuner.
We are going to have breakfast.

(zhuh prahN luh traN)
Je prends le train.
I'm taking the train.

(tew vuh prahN druhN vehr)
Tu veux prendre un verre?
Do you want to have a drink?

CHAPTER 2

J'ai faim!
I'm hungry!

French is thought of as a "nasal" language because it has nasal vowels. Believe it or not, there are only 4 nasal vowels you have to learn in French. Look at the phrase ***un bon vin blanc*** (*uN bohN vaN blahNk* – a good white wine): There is an "n" in each word, which tells you that the vowel before it is a nasal vowel. Instead of pronouncing the "n", just try putting the preceding vowel in your nose. Pinch your nose and say "oh" (through your nose). Now put a "b" in front of the "oh" and you have said ***bon***. (Remember... don't pronounce the "n".) Whenever you see an "n" or an "m" think "nose". Exception: two m's or n's together – ***femme*** (fahm), ***homme*** (ohm).

(kehl shahNs)
Quelle chance!
What luck!

(zhay faN)
J'ai faim!
I'm hungry!

VOCABULARY

(ahNtr)
entre
enter

(sor)
sort
leave

(kohN-tahN)
content
happy

(treest)
triste
sad

(ah-mee)
amie
female friend

(fro-mahzh)
fromage
cheese

(dun)
donne
give

NUMBERS

If you want to understand a room number, tell someone your phone number, or understand how much something is you are considering buying, you need numbers. Try to memorize the numbers 0–10 now. (Practice counting throughout the day!) More numbers will be introduced in later chapters.

0	1	2	3	4	5
(zay-roh)	*(uhN)*	*(duh)*	*(trwah)*	*(kahtr)*	*(saNk)*
zéro	un	deux	trois	quatre	cinq

6	7	8	9	10
(sees)	*(set)*	*(weet)*	*(nuhf)*	*(dees)*
six	sept	huit	neuf	dix

NUMBER PRACTICE

Write the answers to these simple arithmetic problems in words.

1. trois + un = _quatre_

2. six + quatre = _dix_

3. deux + trois = _cinq_

4. huit – cinq = _trois_

5. neuf – huit = _un_

6. dix – trois = _sept_

7. quatre x deux = _huit_

8. trois x trois = _neuf_

STORY

(ahn ay sohN nah-mee zhew-lee sohN dahN zuhN kah-fay)
Anne et son amie Julie sont dans un café.
    and her   *are*   *in* *a*

(sahN-ndwee choh froh-mahzh)
Anne mange un sandwich au fromage.

(ah duh sahN-ndwee shoh froh-mahzh)
Julie a deux sandwichs au fromage.
    has

(zhah kahNtr dahN luh kah-fay)
Jacques entre dans le café.
 enters in the

(pray-zahNt)   *(ah)*   *(ahN-shahN-tay dee zhahk)*
Anne présente Jacques à Julie. "Enchanté", dit Jacques.
 introduces   *to*   *Pleased to meet you.*

(pwee ahn dmahN dah zhahk seel ah faN)
Puis Anne demande à Jacques s'il a faim.
then   *asks*   *if he is hungry*

(eel ray-pohN wee zhay fahN)
Il répond "Oui, j'ai faim!"
     yes

(lwee dohn uhN sahN-dweesh)
Julie lui donne un sandwich.
   him

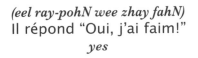

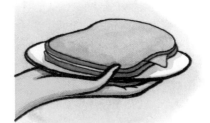

(mehr-see kehl shahNs)
"Merci. Quelle chance!" répond Jacques.
thank you

(ee lay treh kohN-tahN)   *(dee zhuh voo zahn pree)*
Il est très content. Julie lui dit "Je vous en prie."
  is very   *tells him you're welcome*

PRACTICE

The statements below are all false. Change each one to make it true.

1. Anne et son amie mangent dans la voiture.

   _____

2. Julie a trois sandwichs. _____

3. Jacques sort du café. _____

4. Jacques est triste. _____

VERB FOCUS

(ehtr)	
être	
to be	

(zhuh swee kohN-tahN(t)
Je suis content(e).
I am happy.

(tew eh kohN-tahN(t))
Tu es content.
You are happy.

(ehl eh kohN-tahNt)
Elle est contente.
She is happy.

(eel eh kohN-tahN)
Il est content.
He is happy.

(noo sohm treest)
Nous sommes tristes.
We are sad.

(voo zeht treest)
Vous êtes tristes.
You are sad.

(ehl sohN treest)
Elles sont tristes.
They (female) are sad.

(eel sohN treest)
Ils sont tristes.
They (male) are sad.

Here are some useful sentences with the verb "be":

(ehl eh dohk-tuhr/proh-feh-suhr/ahr-teest)
Elle est docteur/professeur/artiste.
She is a doctor/teacher/artist.

(lah vah-leez nwah reh tah mwah)
La valise noire est à moi.
The black suitcase is mine.

(shuh swee dah-kohr)
Je suis d'accord.
I agree.

(eel sohN tahN traN dmahN-zhay)
Ils sont en train de manger.
They are busy eating.

(oh neh tahN ruh-tahr)
On est en retard.
We are late.

CHAPTER 3

(Ehk-skew-zay mwah)
Excusez–moi!
Excuse me! Sorry!

If you are traveling to a foreign country, there will be many opportunities for you to start a conversation with native speakers of the language. Don't be shy! Of course some people will be in a hurry or won't want to talk to you. However, many people will be interested to meet someone traveling in their country. You'll want to learn some basic questions and appropriate responses as well as some useful expressions.

(zhay swahf)
J'ai soif.
I'm thirsty.

(zhuh swee fah-tee-gay)
Je suis fatigué.
I'm tired.

(suh neh pah grahv)
Ce n'est pas grave.
That's OK. Don't worry about it.
It's not serious.

VOCABULARY

(wee)
oui
yes

(duh)
de (d')
from

(oo)
où
where

(vyaN)
viens
come

(pahrl)
parle
speak

(uhN puh)
un peu
a little

(zhuh mah-pehl)
je m'appelle
my name is

(vwah-see)
voici
here is

USEFUL EXPRESSIONS

Here are some ways to say yes and no:

(wee)
OUI!
yes

(nohN)
NON!
no

(seh sa)
C'est ça!
That's right!

(meh wee)
Mais oui!
Certainly!

(byaN sewr)
Bien sûr!
Sure! Of course!

(ah nohN)
Ah, non!
No way!

(meh nohN)
Mais non!
Of course not!

(o kohN trehr)
Au contraire!
On the contrary!

DIALOG

Sometimes bumping into people by accident can lead to introductions and even friendships. Read what *Dan et Sylvie* have to say to each other after they bump into one another on the street.

Dan Duncan: l'homme   **Sylvie Simonet:** la femme   **Sophie:** la fille   **David:** le garçon *(luh gahr-sohN)*

1.   **Dan:** Excusez-moi!   **Sylvie:** Ce n'est pas grave.

2.   **Dan:** *(voo zeht frahN-sehz)* Vous êtes française?   **Sylvie:** *(doo vuh-nay voo)* Oui! D'où venez-vous?
     Are you French?

    Dan: Je viens de Seattle, Washington.   *(kohN-mahN voo zah-play voo)*
          Je m'appelle Dan Duncan. Et vous?   Comment vous appelez-vous?

3.   **Sylvie:** Je m'appelle Sylvie Simonet.   *(zhuh voo pray-zahNt mah fee-y)* Je vous présente ma fille, Sophie.

4.   **Dan:** *(sah-lew)* *(keh lahzh ah-tew)* Salut, Sophie. Quel âge as-tu?   **Sophie:** J'ai 8 ans.

5.   **Dan:** *(mohN fees)* Voici mon fils, David. Il parle un peu français.

    Sophie: Bonjour, David. Quel âge as-tu?

6.   **David:** J'ai 5 ans et j'ai faim et j'ai soif et suis fatigué.

N O T E :   Notice the use of *"tu"* with the boy and girl and *"vous"* with the adult. Look back at Chapter 1 for the explanation of this rule.

PRACTICE

Study the dialog. Then, see if you can write the missing question. The response is given.

1. _____ ? J'ai 10 ans.

2. _____ ? Je viens de Boston.

3. _____ ? Je m'appelle Sylvie Simonet.

4. _____ ? Oui! Je suis américain.

*Note: A woman would say *Je suis américaine (zhuh swee zah-may-ree-kehn)*. A French woman says *Je suis française (zhuh swee frahN-sehz)*. A French man says *Je suis français (frahN-seh)*. A woman from *Québec (kay-behk)*: *Je suis québécoise (kay-bay-kwaz)*. A man from *Québec: Je suis québécois (kay-bay-kwah)*.

ASKING QUESTIONS IN FRENCH

A. The easiest way to ask a question in French is to simply raise your voice at the end of a sentence.

(voo zeht frahN-sehz)
Vous êtes française?
You're French?

(ay voo)
Et vous?
And you?

B. Another way is to invert the subject and the verb. (Put the pronoun after the verb.)

(doo vuh-nay voo)
D'où venez–vous?
Where do you come from?

(kohN-mahN voo zah-play voo)
Comment vous appelez–vous?
What's your name?

(keh lahzh ah-tew)
Quel âge as–tu?
How old are you?

C. Still another way is to put *Est-ce que (ehs-kuh)* "Is it that" at the beginning of the sentence. The order of the words stays the same.

(ehs kuh voo zeht fah-tee-gay)
Est–ce que vous êtes fatigué?
Are you tired?

(ehs kuh zhuh mahzh tro)
Est–ce que je mange trop?
Do I eat/am I eating too much?

PRACTICE

Now practice asking questions. Write a question using the method indicated (A, B, or C), putting the words in the correct order.

Ex: <u>français</u> /parlez/vous (A)

(voo pahr-lay frahN seh)
<u>Vous parlez français?</u>_____?

1. êtes/vous/français (C) _____?

2. faim/tu/as (A) _____?

3. avez/faim/vous (C) _____?

4. venez/d'où/vous (B) _____?

5. vous/mangez/les escargots (B) _____?

6. vous/quel âge/avez (A) _____?

AVOIR
to have

j'ai	*(zhay)*	*I have*
tu as	*(tew ah)*	*you have*
il, elle, on a	*(eel, ehl, ohN ah)*	*he, she, one has*
nous avons	*(noo zah-vohN)*	*we have*
vous avez	*(voo zah-vay)*	*you have*
ils, elles ont	*(eel, ehl zohN)*	*they have*

Notice that many expressions in French with *avoir* + noun are expressed in English with be + adjective:

"I am thirsty" becomes *J'ai soif* (I have thirst).

Notice also that the French use *avoir* to state their age:

J'ai 10 ans rather than "I am 10 years old." However… *Je SUIS fatigué.*

Here are some other useful expressions with the verb *"avoir"*:

(zhay buh-zwaN duh)	*(tewah duh lah shahNs)*	*(zhay puhr)*
J'ai besoin de…	Tu as de la chance.	J'ai peur.
I need…	*You're lucky.*	*I'm afraid.*

(voo zah-vay reh-zohN)	*(zhay soh-mehy)*	*(voo zah-vay tohr)*
Vous avez raison.	J'ai sommeil.	Vous avez tort.
You're right.	*I'm sleepy.*	*You're wrong.*

PARLER
to speak

je parle	*(zhuh pahrl)*	*I speak*
tu parles	*(tew pahrl)*	*you speak*
il, elle, on parle	*(eel, ehl ohN pahrl)*	*he, she, one speaks*
		(we speak)
nous parlons	*(noo pahr-lohN)*	*we speak*
vous parlez	*(voo pahr-lay)*	*you speak*
ils, elles parlent	*(eel, ehl pahrl)*	*they speak*

CHAPTER 4

(kohN-byaN sa koot)
Combien ça coûte?
How much is it?

VOCABULARY

(keh-skuh)
Qu'est–ce que
what

(meh)
mais
but

(dahN)
dans
in

(da-kohr)
D'accord!
OK! Agreed!

(vwah-lah)
voilà
There you are. There it is.

(plew)
plus
more

(lahN-tmahN)
lentement
slowly

(ewn boo-lahN zhree)
une boulangerie
a bakery

(kohN-prahN)
comprends
understand

(voo-dreh)
voudrais
would like

(ewn boo-tehy do mee-nay-rahl)
une bouteille d'eau minérale
a bottle of mineral water

BE POLITE

(swah poh-lee)
Sois poli!
Be polite!

(mehr-see byaN)   *(bo-koo)*
merci bien *or* merci beaucoup
thank you very much

(nohN mehr-see)
non, merci
no thank you

(seel voo pleh)
s'il vous plaît *(formal)*
please

(duh ryaN)
de rien *(informal)*
you're welcome

(zhuh voo zahN pree)
je vous en prie
you're welcome

(seel tuh pleh)
s'il te plaît *(informal)*
please

(nohN mehr-see)
non, merci
no thank you

(o ruh-vwahr)
au revoir
good bye

Note: *Madame (mah-dahm)* (Mrs.) is used for older women, whether they are married or not. *Mademoiselle (mah-dmwah-zehl)* (Miss, Ms) is used for younger women.

Monsieur (muh-syuh) is used for men. *Messieurs-dames (meh-syuh-dahm)* (ladies and gentlemen) is very commonly used in formal situations when one or more women and men are addressed.

These titles are used a great deal in formal conversations and without the names of the people, even if the names are known:

Bonjour, madame.   Au revoir, monsieur.

STORY

(eel eh dee zuhr dew mah-taN)
Il est dix heures du matin.

(ee-zah-beh lay zhahN sohN tah pah-ree)
Isabelle et Jean sont à Paris.

(frahN-sehs)
Isabelle est française.

(eh tah-meh-ree-kaN meh)
John est américain mais il parle un
                           but

(frahN-seh) (eel sohN dahN zewn)
peu français. Ils sont dans une boulangerie.
                      in

(vahN-duhz)   *(bohN-zhoor)*
Vendeuse: Bonjour, messieurs–dames.

Isabelle: Bonjour, madame.

John: Bonjour, madame.

(keh-skuh voo day-zee-ray)
Vendeuse: Qu'est–ce que vous désirez?
What do you want?

(zhuh voo-dreh ewn bah-geht seel-voo-pleh)
Isabelle: Je voudrais une baguette, s'il vous plaît.
              long loaf of bread

(ay voo)   (muh-syuh)
Vendeuse: Et vous, monsieur?

           Qu'est–ce que vous désirez?

(zhuh nuh kohN-prahN pah pahr-lay plew)
John: Je ne comprends pas. Parlez plus
         I don't understand   speak

         lentement, s'il vous plaît.
         slowly

(dah-kohr)
Vendeuse: D'accord. Qu'est–ce que vous désirez?
         ok
                (duh zay-klehr o shoh-koh-lah)
John: Je voudrais deux éclairs au chocolat, s'il vous plaît.

	(vwah-lah)
Vendeuse:	Voilà.

	(voo zah-vay duh lo mee-nay-rahl)
Isabelle:	Vous avez de l'eau minérale?

	(byaN sewr)
Vendeuse:	Bien sûr, mademoiselle.
	of course

	(ewn boo-tehy) (do mee-nay-rahl)
	Voilà. Une bouteille d'eau minérale.

	(kohN-byaN sa koot)
Isabelle:	Merci bien, madame. Combien ça coûte?

	(trwa zyuh-ro)
Vendeuse:	Trois euros, s'il vous plaît.
	euro

Isabelle:	Voilà trois euros.
Vendeuse:	Merci, mademoiselle.

	(o ruh-vwahr)
John et Isabelle:	Au revoir, madame.

Vendeuse:	Au revoir, messieurs–dames.

DO YOU UNDERSTAND?

Read the dialog carefully and see if you can answer these questions. Answer in French or English. Check your answers in the back of the book.

1. Who is French in this dialog? _____

2. Why doesn't John understand? _____

3. What does John want to buy? _____

4. Who asks for mineral water? _____

5. Where does this scene take place? _____

NUMERAUX 11 - 22

11	12	13	14	15	16
(ohNz) onze	*(dooz)* douze	*(trehz)* treize	*(kah-torze)* quatorze	*(kahz)* quinze	*(sehz)* seize

17	18	19	20	21	22
(dee-seht) dix–sept	*(dee-zweet)* dix–huit	*(dee-znuhf)* dix–neuf	*(vaN)* vingt	*(vaN tay uhN)* vingt et un	*(vaN-duh)* vingt–deux

WHAT WOULD YOU LIKE?

(keh-skuh voo day-zee-ray)
Qu'est–ce que vous désirez?
What would you like? or How can I help you?

Je voudrais is the polite (conditional) form of the verb *vouloir* "to want" and is commonly used, but it's always good to say "please" – *s'il vous plaît* at the beginning or end of the sentence too.

Write the numbers in words, just for practice. Say the numbers out loud as you write them. Then practice saying each sentence with *s'il vous plaît.* at the end.
For example: *Je voudrais deux éclairs au chocolat, s'il vous plaît.*

(zhuh voo-dreh)   *(kahrt po-stahl)*
1. Je voudrais _____ cartes postales.
    I would like   11

                      (taNbr)
2. Je voudrais _____ timbres.
                 18

                      (bee-yeh)
3. Je voudrais _____ billets.
                 15

(ohN)   *(kah-fay)*
4. On voudrait _____ cafés.
   we   3

                      (stee-lo)
5. Je voudrais _____ stylos.
                 5

      (boo-tehy do mee-nay-rahl)
6. On voudrait _____ bouteilles d'eau minerale.
                 2

CHAPTER 5

(kehl zhoor sohm-noo)
Quel jour sommes–nous?
What day is it?

(luh koo duh foodr)
le coup de foudre
love at first sight

(lah fluhr)
la fleur
flower

(ahN-new-yuh/ahN-new-yuhz)
ennuyeux/ennuyeuse
boring

(too lay duh)
tous les deux
both

(ah-vwahr luh sahN sho)
avoir le sang chaud
to be quick-tempered

VOCABULARY

(luh zhar-daN)
le jardin
garden

(maN tnahN)
maintenant
now

(mah-rahN/mah-rahNt)
marrant/marrante
funny

(luh proh-grah-muhr)
le programmeur
computer programmer

(lah meh-zohN)
la maison
house

(lah vwa-tewr)
la voiture
car

(eh-may)
aimer
to like/love

(lay zyuh)
les yeux
eyes

(saN-pah-teek)
sympathique
nice

(lay-twahl)
l'étoile
star

FOCUS : VERBS

French verbs are either "regular", if the endings you add to the main part of the word follow a set pattern, or "irregular" if they don't.

There are three types of "regular" French verbs:

-er   (like *manger* – to eat and *parler* – to speak) These end in –er.

-ir   (like *finir* – to finish and *choisir* – to choose) These end in –ir.

-re   (like *vendre* – to sell and *attendre* – to wait for) These end in –re.

Most verbs in French are "regular", so all you have to do is learn the endings that go with the three different forms (-er, -ir, and -re) if you want to write them. If you only want to say them, it's even easier. In all regular verbs and in many irregular ones, the first three conjugations *(je, tu, il/elle/on)* are pronounced exactly the same. In the -er type, the *ils/elles* conjugation is also pronounced like the first three just mentioned.

Here is what to do if you want to conjugate *parler* or other verbs that end in –er:
you just take off the -er, which leaves the stem *parl-*.
Now add the endings: *je, tu, il/elle/on: -e, -es, e*
                                          nous, vous, ils/elles: -ons, -ez, -ent

This introductory book focuses on the –er verbs because it is the largest of the three types. Warning! When you conjugate "manger", you must add an "e" to "nous man<u>ge</u>ons" keeping the soft sound of the "g".

Here is an example of a regular -er verb conjugation:

(ah-bee-tay)
HABITER
to live

j'habite	*(zhah-beet)*	*I live*
tu habites	*(tew ah-beet)*	*you live*
il, elle, on habite	*(eel, ehl, ohN (n)ah-beet)*	*he, she, one lives*
nous habitons	*(noo zah-bee-tohN)*	*we live*
vous habitez	*(voo zah-bee-tay)*	*you live*
ils, elles habitent	*(eel, ehl zah-beet)*	*they live*

See page 32 for French colors.

(ah-laN ay mah-ree ah-bee tewn grahNd meh-zohN)
Alain et Marie habitent une grande maison bleue et rose.

(eel zohN tuhN puh-tee)   *(day fluhr roo zheh zhon)*
Ils ont un petit jardin avec des fleurs rouges et jaunes.
they have

(eh)
Alain est programmeur.

(eel ah   ahN ay ah lay zyuh vehr)
Il a 25 ans et a les yeux verts.
            has   *green*

(treh   saN-pah-teek   meh)
Il est très sympathique, mais
      very

(kehl-kuh-fwa eel a luh sahN sho)
quelquefois il a le sang chaud.
sometimes

(fahm dah-fehr)
Marie est une femme d'affaires.
            businesswoman

(lay zyuh mah-rohN)
Elle a 26 ans et a les yeux marron.

Elle est marrante.

(poor tou lay duh)   *(seh-teh luh koo)*
Pour tous les deux, c'était le coup
for both of them   *it was love*

(duh foodr)
de foudre.
at first sight

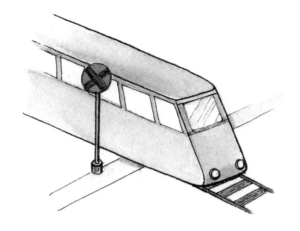

(too lay duh   sohn treh zoh-kew-pay)
Tous les deux sont très occupés.

(shahk   luhN-dee)   (vah)   (ahN traN)
Chaque lundi, Marie va à Paris en train.
each   Monday   goes to

(mehr-kruh-dee)   (vwah-tewr)
Chaque mercredi Alain va à Marseille en voiture.
each   Wednesday

(meh)   (vahN-druh-dee)   (mahN zhahN-sahNbl)
Mais chaque vendredi Alain et Marie mangent ensemble
but   Friday   together

(dahN luh reh-sto-rahN kee)   (lay-twahl roozh)
dans le restaurant qui s'appelle "L'Etoile Rouge".
                which is called   the red star

PRACTICE

Complete the sentences in English or French (or both!). Use the vocabulary and the dialog to help you.

1. Alain and Marie live in a big blue and pink _____.

2. Alain is 25 _____.

3. Alain is very _____.

4. Marie is _____.

5. Alain doesn't like his _____.

6. Marie goes to Paris by _____.

7. Alain goes to Marseille by _____.

(blahN)
blanc
white

(bluh)
bleu
blue

(gree)
gris
gray

(mah-rohN)
marron
brown

(nwahr)
noir
black

(oh-rahNzh)
orange
orange

(zhon)
jaune
yellow

(vehr)
vert
green

(roz)
rose
pink

(roozh)
rouge
red

PRACTICE

(lay koo-luhr)
LES COULEURS

See how many colors you can remember.
Fill in the crossword puzzle with the French
words for the colors.

DOWN

1. yellow
2. blue
3. pink
4. orange
5. white

ACROSS

3. red
6. grey
7. brown
8. green

DAYS OF THE WEEK

(lay zhoor duh lah suh-mehn)
les jours de la semaine

Notice that the days of the week are not capitalized in French and they are all masculine. In addition, French calendars begin with Monday (not Sunday, like ours).

(luhN-dee)	*(mahr-dee)*	*(mehr-kruh-dee)*	*(zhuh-dee)*	*(vahN-druh-dee)*	*(sahm-dee)*	*(dee-mahNsh)*
lundi	mardi	mercredi	jeudi	vendredi	samedi	dimanche
Monday	*Tuesday*	*Wednesday*	*Thursday*	*Friday*	*Saturday*	*Sunday*

Find *les jours de la semaine* hidden in the puzzle. Then circle them.

u	a	c	x	w	s	c	s	l	i
i	d	e	r	d	n	e	v	s	d
i	d	n	u	l	m	p	x	a	u
v	n	r	c	z	g	p	g	m	e
d	i	m	a	n	c	h	e	e	j
q	c	s	c	m	q	u	a	d	i
m	e	r	c	r	e	d	i	i	r

PRACTICE

Put *les jours de la semaine* in order beginning with Monday by putting a number from 1 to 7 in front of each day.

_____ mercredi   _____ dimanche   _____ mardi   _____ vendredi

_____ lundi   _____ samedi   _____ jeudi

CHAPTER 6

(seh lwaN)
C'est loin?
Is it far?

Understanding directions in another language is particularly difficult, but not impossible! Of course it helps to have *une carte* (a map) so you can look at the names of the streets as the person you ask points to them. You don't have to understand every *mot* (word).

(mahr-shay)
marchez
walk

(pruh-nay)
prenez
take

(fehr-may/fehr-may)
fermé/fermée
closed

(oo-vehr/ouvehrt)
ouvert/ouverte
open

(seh proh-mnay)
se promener
to go for a walk

(preh duh)
près de
near

LISTEN FOR THE VERBS.
This will generally be the first word you hear because it will be in the command form: Walk, Take, Go, Turn, Go up, Go down, Cross.

LISTEN FOR THE DIRECTION WORDS.
right, left, straight ahead, next to, on the other side of, facing

LISTEN FOR THE NAMES OF THE STREETS.
These will be the hardest to understand. You can learn verbs and directions in advance, but names of people and places are more difficult because of the differences in pronunciation between English and French.

(lwaN)
loin
far

(mohN-tay)
montez
go up

(day-sahN-day)
descendez
go down

(leh pohN)
le pont
bridge

In Chapter 5 you learned how to conjugate "regular" verbs – those that have a set pattern of endings. The verb *aller* (to go) conjugated at the bottom of this page is an example of an "irregular" verb, (although since it ends in "er", it looks like a "regular verb). Since there is no pattern to the endings for "irregular" verbs, these forms must be memorized. Other examples of irregular verbs you have studied so far in this book are: *être* (to be), *avoir* (to have), and *prendre* (to take). (Although *prendre* looks like a regular –re verb, it has irregular endings in the plural forms: *prends, prends, prend, prenons, prenez, prennent*.) Try to memorize *aller*. It's a very useful verb! Just say them out loud in the order given in the box from the top (beginning with *je vais*).

(duh lotre ko-tay duh)
de l'autre côté de
on the other side (of)

(ah ko-tay duh)
à côté de
next to

(ahN fahs duh)
en face de
facing

(ah gohsh)
à gauche
to the left

(too drwah)
tout droit
straight ahead

(ah drwaht)
à droite
to the right

(ah-lay)
ALLER
to go

je vais	*(zhuh veh)*	*I go*
tu vas	*(tew vah)*	*you go*
il, elle, on va	*(eel, ehl, ohN vah)*	*he, she one goes*
nous allons	*(noo zah-lohN)*	*we go*
vous allez	*(voo zah-lay)*	*you go*
ils, elles vont	*(eel, ehl vohN)*	*they go*

ORDINAL NUMBERS

You will need to know ordinal numbers when someone gives you directions (telling you which *rue* to turn on). These numbers also come in handy when you need to tell which *étage* (floor) your *chambre d'hôtel* (hotel room) is on, or which *étage* you want to stop on in a *grand magasin* (department store).

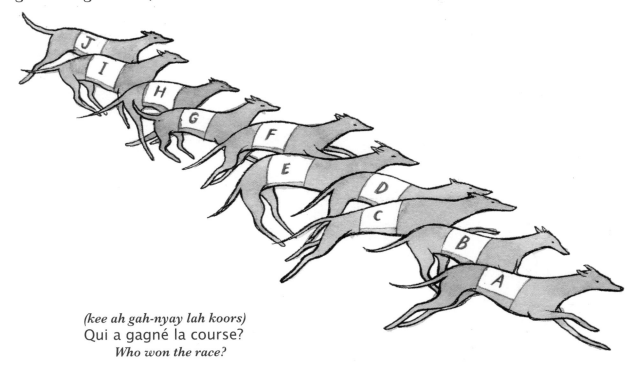

(kee ah gah-nyay lah koors)
Qui a gagné la course?
Who won the race?

Using the numbers on the right, fill in the blanks to help the race announcer announce the winning *chien (syaN = dog)* and the first nine runner–ups. Say each number as you write it. Notice the differences in spelling in *cin<u>qu</u>ième and neu<u>v</u>ième*.

A is _____	F is _____	*(nuh-vyem)* neuvième	*(seh-tyem)* septième
B is _____	G is _____	*(kah-tree-yem)* quatrième	*(wee-tyem)* huitième
C is _____	H is _____	*(pruh-myay)* premier (première)	*(dee-zyem)* dixième
D is _____	I is _____	*(see-zyem)* sixième	*(duh-zyem)* deuxième
E is _____	J is _____	*(saN-kyem)* cinquième	*(trwah-zyem)* troisième

DIALOG

(mee-shehl ay nee-kohl)   *(uhN no-tehl)*
Michel et Nicole are standing outside *un hôtel* talking.

(oo vah tew oh-zhoor-dwee)
Michel: Où vas–tu aujourd'hui?
       go

(zhuh veh o see-nay-mah)
Nicole: Je vais au cinéma.
       to the

(Meh)   *(seh laN-dee)*   *(eh fehr-may)*
Michel: Mais aujourd'hui c'est lundi. Le cinéma est fermé.
 but   *closed*

(wee   seh vreh)   (tahN-pee   eh twah)
Nicole: Oui, c'est vrai. Tant pis! Et toi, où vas–tu?
 that's right   too bad   and you

Michel: (dah-bohr)   (ah lah bahNk ahN-sweet)   (fehr day koors)   (dahN zuhN grahN)

(dah-bohr)   *(ah lah bahNk ahN-sweet)*   *(fehr day koors)*   *(dahN zuhN grahN)*

Michel: D'abord je vais à la banque. Ensuite, je vais faire des courses dans un grand
first   *then*   *to go shopping*   *in*   *department*

(mah-gah-zaN) (vuh) (vuh-neer)
magasin. Veux–tu venir avec moi?
store   *to come*

                              (zhuh pahNs kuh zhehm-ray ah-lay vee-zee-tay uhN mew-zay dahr)

Nicole: Non, merci. Je pense que j'aimerais aller visiter un musée d'art.
                         that I would like to go

(puh)   *(dohr-say)*   *(eel eh-too-vehr)*

Michel: Tu peux aller au Musée d'Orsay aujourd'hui. Il est ouvert le lundi.
    can   *it*   *open*

(zhay-nyahl oo-weh)   *(seh lwaN)*

Nicole: Génial! Où est le Musée d'Orsay? C'est loin?
    great

(seh neh pah)   *(vah too drwah)*   *(prahN)*   *(preh-myehr rew ah gohsh)*

Michel: Non, ce n'est pas loin… Va tout droit et prend la première rue à gauche.
    it is not   *go*

(seh)   *(raN-bo)*   *(kohN-tee-new zhew-sko boo-lvahr ah-nah-tohl frahNs)*
C'est la rue de Rimbaud. Continue jusqu'au boulevard Anatole France.
                     until

(toorn ah drwaht)   *(pohN day zah-moo-ruh)*
Ensuite, tourne à droite. Continue jusqu'au pont des Amoureux.
                     bridge of the lovers

(trah-vehrs)   *(ee-may-dee-aht-mahN)*
Traverse le pont et tourne immédiatement à gauche.
cross

(tew veh-rah)   *(sewr tah)*
Tu verras le musée sur ta droite.
   will see   *on your*

(dah-kohr)   *(ah byaN-to)*
Nicole: D'accord. Merci, Michel. A bientôt!
           see you later

Michel: A bientôt! Bonne promenade!
      have a good walk

PRACTICE

Comprenez–vous?
Do you understand?

Répondez "oui" ou "non".

1. Est–ce que le cinéma est fermé le mercredi? _____
2. Est–ce que le Musée d'Orsay est ouvert le lundi? _____
3. Est–ce que Nicole veut faire des courses aujourd'hui? _____
4. Est–ce loin d'aller au Musée d'Orsay? _____

(kehl eh tah say-zohN pray-fay-ray)
Quelle est ta saison préférée?
Which season do you prefer?

(ahN dotr moh)
en d'autres mots
in other words

(mwah-o-see)
moi aussi
me too

(ah mohN nah-vee)
à mon avis
in my opinion

(too luh mohNd)
tout le monde
everyone

(duh tahN zahN tahN)
de temps en temps
from time to time

LES SAISONS DE L'ANNÉE

(lay seh-zohN duh lah-nay)
the seasons of the year

Notice that *le printemps* (spring) is different from the other seasons when you want to express "in" before the season.

(zhuh veh ah moN-ray-all ahN-nay-tay)
Je vais à Montréal en été.
I'm going to Montreal in the summer.

(zhuh veh zahN behl-zhee kahN-nee-vehr)
Je vais en Belgique en hiver.
I'm going to Belgium in the winter.

(zhun veh ah la mar-tee-nee kahN-no-tohn)
Je vais à la Martinique en automne.
I'm going to Martinique in autumn (the fall).

(zhuh veh ah nee soh praN-tahN)
Je vais à Nice au printemps.
I'm going to Nice in the spring.

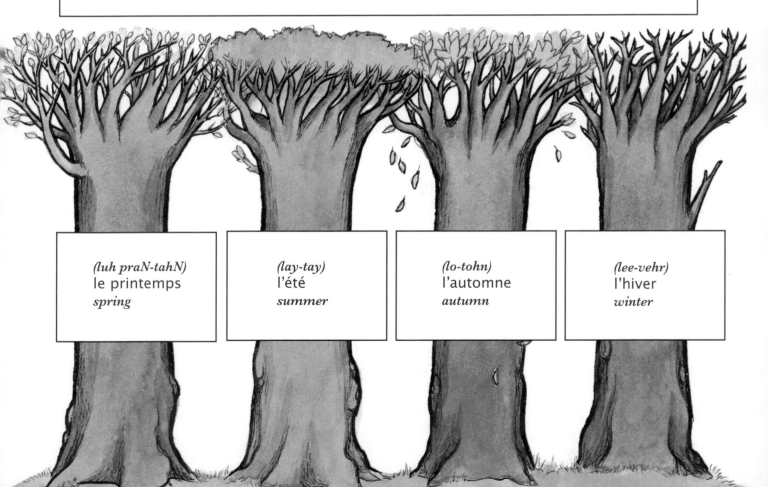

(luh praN-tahN)
le printemps
spring

(lay-tay)
l'été
summer

(lo-tohn)
l'automne
autumn

(lee-vehr)
l'hiver
winter

LES MOIS DE L'ANNÉE

(lay mwah duh lah-nay)
the months of the year

Say each month out loud in French, using the pronunciation key. Try not to read them as you would in English. Remember not to say the "n's" or "m's" as we do in English. The capital *N* means "Put it in your nose." You should feel a slight vibration through your nose when you say a nasal vowel. Drop your jaw (which opens your mouth) when you see *ahN*, and don't close it until you get to the next sound: *day-sahN* (mouth open) *br* (mouth closed) for *décembre*. Notice that the months are not capitalized in French.

(zhahN-vyay)
janvier

(fay-vree-ay)
février

(mahrs)
mars

(ah-vreel)
avril

(meh)
mai

(zhwaN)
juin

(zhwee-yeh)
juillet

(oot)
août

(sehp-tahNbr)
septembre

(ok-tohbr)
octobre

(noh-vahNbr)
novembre

(day-sahNbr)
décembre

STORY

Look at the pictures and read the sentences under each one. See if you can figure out *le sens* (*luh sahNs* = the meaning). Write what you think the sentences mean in the blanks. Use the vocabulary and idioms on the previous pages to help you *comprendre* (*kohN-prahNdr* = to understand) the story that follows the pictures.

(lah mehr)	*(luh pehr)*	*(lah suhr)*	*(luh frehr)*
la mère	le père	la soeur	le frère
mother	*father*	*sister*	*brother*

(lah mehr eh tah lah plazh ahN nay-tay)
La mère est à la plage en été.

1. _____

(luh pehr eh dahN lay mohN-tah nyahN nee-vehr)
Le père est dans les montagnes en hiver.

2. _____

(luh frehr rahN-dohn nahN noh-tohn)
Le frère randonne en automne.

3. _____

(lay suhr ruh-gard lay fluhr oh prahN-tahN)
Les soeurs regardent les fleurs au printemps.

4. _____

(zhuh mah-pehl ee-rehn shah-boh   zhay vaN tahN   zhay ewn fah-mee-y   treh zaN-tay-reh-sahNt)
Je m'appelle Irène Chabot. J'ai 20 ans. J'ai une famille très intéressante. Nous

(sohm)   (toos)   *(kahN noo pruh-nohN   day va-kahNs) (mah)*   *(vuh too-zhoor)*
sommes tous différents. Quand nous prenons des vacances, ma mère veut toujours
   are   *all*   *when*   *wants always*

(ah-lay ah lah plazh)   *(lay mohN-tah-nyuh)*
aller à la plage, mais mon père aime les montagnes. En d'autres mots, ma mère aime

(ahN nay-tay sewr-too ahN oot) (mohN)   *(lee-vehr) (ee lehm skee-yay)*
prendre des vacances en été, surtout en août. Mon père préfère l'hiver. Il aime skier
                        especially

(ehm rahN-duh-nay)
en décembre ou en janvier. Mon frère, Robert, qui a 17 ans, aime randonner en
                                                              to hike
(fo-reh)   *(koo-luhr)*   *(lo-tohm)*   *(dohNk)*
forêt. Il aime les couleurs de l'automne (orange, rouge, jaune, marron). Donc, il
                                                                so
(vuh prahNdr)   *(ahN)*   *(oo)*   *(puh-teet)*
veut prendre des vacances en septembre ou octobre. Ma petite soeur Janine, 15
                                          or
(ahN)   *(ehmohN) (lay) (behl fluhr)*
ans, aime le printemps. Moi aussi! Janine et moi aimons les belles fleurs.

(cuh-pahN-dahN)   *(nehm pah)*   *(sohN)*
Cependant, ma soeur n'aime pas voyager. A mon avis, mars, avril et mai sont les
however

(plew bo)   *(poor)*   *(kahN   pruh-nohN noo noh)*   *(too-to lohN)*
plus beaux mois pour voyager. Quand prenons–nous nos vacances? Tout au long de
most beautiful   *for*   *our*

(lah-nay)   (noo rahN-doh-nohN)
l'année! Nous randonnons chaque samedi en septembre. De temps en temps, nous

(o-see ahN nee-vehr)   *(byaN sewr)*   *(skee-yohN   wee-kehnd)*
randonnons aussi en hiver et au printemps. Bien sûr, nous skions les week–ends en
                                        of course

(oot   noo zah-lohn soo-vahN)
décembre, janvier et février. En juin, juillet et août, nous allons souvent à la plage.
                                                often

(reh-stohN oh-see)   *(may-zohN) (aN-see too-luh-mohNd)*
Nous restons aussi souvent à la maison. Ainsi, tout le monde est content.
  stay   *also*   *at home*   *thus everybody*

PRACTICE

A. See if you can translate the following sentences into *anglais*.

1. Mon père préfère l'hiver. _____

2. Mon frère, Robert, qui a 17 ans, aime randonner en forêt.

   _____

3. Quand prenons-nous nos vacances?
   when

   _____

4. De temps en temps, nous randonnons aussi en hiver et au printemps.

   _____

B. Now try to translate these sentences into *français*.

1. I'm 20 years old. _____

2. He likes the colors of autumn (orange, red, yellow, brown).

   _____

3. Me too! Janine and I love the beautiful flowers.

   _____

4. In June, July, and August we often go to the beach.

   _____

FOCUS

All French nouns are either masculine or feminine in gender. Sometimes it's easy to figure out which group a noun belongs to as in *un américain,* an American man, and *une américaine,* an American woman. Other times it just doesn't make any sense: *la cravate* (a necktie) is feminine and *le maquillage* (make-up) is masculine.

Try to learn the noun markers (*le, la, un,* or *une*) together with the nouns: *la plage, la fleur, le printemps, le mois, une famille, un jour.* This will help you a lot in remembering the gender.

FEMININE
la mère

MASCULINE
le père

There are 4 different ways of saying "the" (the definite article):

le, la, l', les

l'automne (masculine, but also is used with feminine nouns that begin with a vowel as in *l'amie* – or an *h* as in *l'heure*)

les vacances (plural – masculine and feminine)

Choose the definite article that goes with each noun.
You may have to look back at previous chapters!

1. _____ soeur

2. _____ plage

3. _____ famille

4. _____ fromage

5. _____ voiture

6. _____ homme

7. _____ matin

8. _____ saison

9. _____ musée

10. _____ rue

There are 2 different ways of saying "a" (the indefinite article):

un mois (masculine), *une maison* (feminine).

Unlike English, French also has a plural form of the indefinite article, *des* (some):

des montagnes, des fleurs

CHAPTER 8

(vwah-see mah fah-mee-y)
Voici ma famille.
This is my family.

There is a good chance that if you make *un ami français* or *une amie française* you will be introduced to some of his or her family members at some point. Not only is it important to be able to understand these words that show family relationships, but it's also useful to be able to introduce and talk about the members of your family.

(luh shah-po)
le chapeau
hat

(day lew-neht)
des lunettes
glasses

(grahN/grahNd)
grand/grande
tall

(lay shuh-vuh)
les cheveux
hair

(lohN/lohNg)
long/longue
long

(puh-tee/puh-teet)
petit/petite
short

(luh mah-ree)
le mari
husband

(lah fahm)
la femme
wife

FOCUS: FAMILY

MALE

le père	(luh pehr)	father
le grand-père	(luh grahN-pehr)	grandfather
le beau-père	(luh bo-pehr)	father-in-law
le frère	(luh frehr)	brother
le beau-frère	(luh bo-frehr)	brother-in law
le fils	(luh fees)	son
le petit-fils	(luh puh-tee-fees)	grandson
l'oncle	(lohNkl)	uncle
le neveu	(luh nuh-vuh)	nephew
le mari	(luh mah-ree)	husband

FEMALE

la mère	(lah mehr)	mother
la grand-mère	(lah grahN- mehr)	grandmother
la belle-mère	(lah behl-mehr)	mother-in-law
la soeur	(lah suhr)	sister
la belle-soeur	(lah behl-suhr)	sister-in-law
la fille	(lah fee-y)	daughter
		("la fille" also means "girl")
la petite-fille	(lah puh-teet fee-y)	granddaughter
la tante	(lah tahNt)	aunt
la nièce	(lah nyehs)	niece
la femme	(lah fahm)	wife

STORY

(pee-yeh-rah ewn puh-teet fa-mee-y sa mehr sah-pehl soh-fee)   (ehl ah day shuh-vuh koor)
Pierre a une petite famille. Sa mère s'appelle Sophie. Elle a des cheveux courts, gris
      has

    (eh)   (dee-nah-meek) (sohN pehr)   (ruh-nay) (eel eh grahN)
et elle est très dynamique. Son père s'appelle René. Il est grand
    is

(ay ehm) (pohr-tay uhN shah-po)   (nah pah duh suhr meh)   (frehr)
et aime porter un chapeau. Pierre n'a pas de soeurs mais il a un frère,
   wear   *doesn't have any*

(pah-treek kee lehm bo-koo)   (mah-rahN)   (mah-ree-yay) (mohr-gahn)
Patrick, qu'il aime beaucoup. Patrick est très marrant.   Il est marié avec Morgane,
      loves   *funny*

    (behl-suhr)   (ah duh lohN shuh-vuh nwahr)
la belle-soeur de Pierre. Elle a de longs cheveux noirs et elle est belle et très sympa.
                              beautiful   *nice*

(eel nohN pas dahN-fahN)   (sah-pehl ay-lehn) (sohN mah-ree)
Ils n'ont pas d'enfants. La belle-mère de Pierre s'appelle Hélène et son mari s'appelle
 don't have any

(ahl-behr)   (bo-pehr)   (lah fahm)   (ahN-dray) (ah day)
Albert. Il est le beau-père de Pierre. La femme de Pierre s'appelle Andrée. Elle a des
                        wife

    (braN) (eh puh-tee tay treh zaN-teh-lee-zhahNt eel zohN tuhN nahN-fahN) (ah-play)
cheveux bruns, est petite et très intelligente. Ils ont un enfant, une fille appelée
                          they have   *girl*

(nah-tah-lee) (ohN zahN)   (sah)   (sewr-too say grahN-pah-rahN)
Nathalie. Elle a 11 ans et adore sa famille, surtout ses grands-parents.   Nathalie

(pohrt day lew-neht)   (bo meh pah treh zaN-teh-lee-gahN)
porte des lunettes. Et Pierre? Il est beau mais pas très intelligent.
wears   *handsome*   *not*

PRACTICE

Fill in the blanks under each picture.
   a) Write the name of the person.
   b) Write what relationship that person is to Pierre. (Be sure to include the definite article *le, la,* or *les* before the word.)

1. a _____
   b _____
2. a _____
   b _____

3. a _____
   b _____
4. a _____
   b _____

(Pierre)

5. a _____
   b _____

6. a _____
   b _____
7. a _____
   b _____

8. a _____
   b _____

Now see if you can answer these questions. Check your answers in the back of the book.

     (kee)
1. Qui est très intelligente? _____
     who
2. Qui a les cheveux courts et gris? _____

3. Qui est marié avec Morgane? _____

4. Qui aime ses grand-parents? _____

5. Qui est beau? _____

FOCUS : ADJECTIVES

In English, adjectives don't change according to the nouns they describe: the tall girl, the tall boy, the tall women – "tall" stays the same. In French, however, the adjective must agree with the noun in gender (masculine or feminine) and number (singular or plural): *la grande fille, le grand garçon, les grandes femmes.*

To make masculine adjectives feminine, you usually had an "e": *court/courte, grand/grande, intelligent/intelligente.* Add "s" to the masculine or feminine form to make the plural *(les grandes femmes).* Short, common adjectives are placed in front of the noun *(petite famille),* but in general, adjectives are placed after the nouns they describe: *une femme intelligente.* This holds true for colors too (chapter 5): *la lune bleue* (the blue moon), *la maison blanche* (the white house – "*blanche*" is an irregular feminine form of "*blanc*"), *les lunettes noires* (the black glasses).

Add the French form of the adjective to each of the nouns:

1. la femme (tall)   <u>la grande femme</u> _____

2. la fille (short)   _____

3. le mari (handsome)   _____

4. la grand-mère (beautiful)   _____

5. la nièce (intelligent)   _____

6. les pères (intelligent)   _____

POSSESSIVE ADJECTIVES

Words like: "my", "your", "his", "her" are possessive adjectives. Just as the definite articles *(le, la, les)* have to agree with the noun, so do the possessive adjectives. Look at the chart on the next page. Notice that in contrast to English, the possessive adjectives in French agree with the thing possessed, not the person who possesses.

A word on pronunciation: in the masculine form with *oncle* you must make the link in pronunciation because *oncle* begins with a vowel: *mon oncle = mohN-nohNkl.* (The "n" sound links to *oncle* so it sounds like one word.)

FEMININE			MASCULINE	
With feminine nouns			*With masculine nouns*	
ma tante	*(mah tahNt)*	MY	mon oncle	*(mohN-nohNkl)*
mes tantes	*(may tahNt)*		mes oncles	*(may-zohNkl)*
ta tante	*(tah tahNt)*	YOUR	ton oncle	*(tohN-nohNkl)*
tes tantes	*(tay tahNt)*	*(familiar)*	tes oncles	*(tay-zohNkl)*
votre tante	*(vohtr tahNt)*	YOUR	votre oncle	*(vo-trohNkl)*
vos tantes	*(vo tahNt)*	*(plural & polite)*	vos oncles	*(vo-zohNkl)*
sa tante	*(sah tahNt)*	HIS/HER	son oncle	*(sohN-nohNkl)*
ses tantes	*(say tahNt)*		ses oncles	*(say-zohNkl)*
notre tante	*(nohtr tahNt)*	OUR	notre oncle	*(no-trohNkl)*
nos tantes	*(no tahNt)*		nos oncles	*(no-zohNkl)*
leur tante	*(luhr tahNt)*	THEIR	leur oncle	*(luh-rohNkl)*
leurs tantes	*(luhr tahNt)*		leurs oncles	*(luhr zohNkl)*

PRACTICE

Now see if you can put the appropriate possessive adjective in front of the following nouns:

1. _____ famille
   my

2. _____ maison
   his

3. _____ père
   her

4. _____ soeur
   your (familiar)

5. _____ frères
   their

6. _____ chapeau
   your (polite)

7. _____ amis
   my

8. _____ mère
   their

9. _____ femme
   his

10. _____ parents
    our

CHAPTER 9

(kehl tahN feh-teel)
Quel temps fait–il?
What's the weather?

Being able to chat about *le temps (luh tahN* - the weather*)* is a useful skill to have in another language. Whether you're at a bus stop, *au restaurant (oh res-toh-rahN),* or making small talk with a desk clerk at a hotel, *le temps* is a safe, popular, topic (and often necessary if you're planning outdoor activities).

A few things to remember: The French do not say "It IS cold" (like we do in English). They use *faire* when they talk about the weather: *Il fait froid.* ("It MAKES cold.") The *il* in weather phrases does not mean "he", nor does it refer to a masculine object. It means "it" as in "It's raining." Notice that *Il pleut* and *Il neige* do not use *faire.*

When you want to say "I AM cold" or "I AM hot" do NOT translate those expressions directly into French (using "am"). Your meaning may be misinterpreted. Instead, say "I HAVE cold" *(J'ai froid – zhay frwah)* or "I HAVE hot" *(J'ai chaud – zhay sho).*

N O T E : You may remember from Chapter 2: *J'ai faim* (I am hungry.) Go back to Chapter 3 to review the different forms of *avoir* (to have) and to see other expressions using *avoir.*

(eel feh sho)
Il fait chaud.
It's hot.

(eel feh frwah)
Il fait froid.
It's cold.

(eel feh dew vahN)
Il fait du vent.
It's windy.

(eel pluh)
Il pleut.
It's raining.

(eel feh dew soh-lay)
Il fait du soleil.
It's sunny.

(eel feh bo)
Il fait beau.
It's beautiful.

(eel feh moh-veh)
Il fait mauvais.
It's horrible.

(eel nehzh)
Il neige.
It's snowing.

DIALOG

This is a telephone conversation between *Elise et sa mère. Elise a 22 ans* and is living in Alaska for 1 year doing research as part of her university graduate studies. *Sa mère* lives in *Paris.*

(bohN-zhoor mah-mahN)
Elise: Bonjour, maman.

(mah shay-ree kohN-mahN vah tew)
Maman: Bonjour, ma chérie. Comment vas–tu?

(zhuh veh byaN sohf kuh zhay frwah)
Elise: Je vais bien sauf que j'ai froid.
     I'm well   except

(mah pohvr puh-teet   eel nehzh)
Maman: Ma pauvre petite…. Il neige?

(seh lee-vehr)   (swee zahN)
Elise: Maman, c'est l'hiver et je suis en Alaska.

(ee-lee-ya)   (ee-see)
Bien sûr, il y a beaucoup de neige ici.
    there is   here

(kehl tahN   feh-teel ah pah-ree)
Quel temps fait–il à Paris?

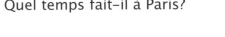

(eel pluh)   (o-zhoor-dwee)
Maman: Il pleut beaucoup aujourd'hui.

(yehr ee-lee-yah-veh dew soh-lehy)
Mais hier, il y avait du soleil. En fait, il
   yesterday, there was   in fact

(fuh-zeh)   (eel feh frwa)
faisait très chaud hier mais il fait froid
it was

(ee-lee-o-rah)   (duh-maN)
aujourd'hui. Il y aura du soleil demain.
    there will be sun   tomorrow

(kahN ruh-vyaN-tew)
Quand reviens-tu à la maison?

53

Elise: *(zhuh nseh pah)* Je ne sais pas. *(byaN oh-kew-pay pahr may ruh-shehrsh)* Je suis bien occupée par mes recherches.
I don't know

(zhuh trah-vahy too lay zhoor sof)
Je travaille tous les jours sauf le dimanche.
work   everyday   except

Maman: Oh mon Dieu! Où travailles–tu?
oh my goodness

Elise: *(prahN lah-vyohN poor)* Je prends l'avion pour Nome tous les
every

(luhN-dee ay zhee rehstsoo-vahN)
lundi et j'y reste souvent deux jours. Je vais souvent
I stay there   often

(ahN vwa-tewr)   *(o-see)* *(seh lwaN dee-see)*
en voiture à Fairbanks aussi. C'est loin d'ici!
from here

(pray-fehr)
Je préfère travailler à Anchorage.

(dwah ruh-toor-nay)   *(suh)*   *(kahN vyaN)*   *(muh rahNdr vee-zeet)*
Je dois retourner à Fairbanks ce vendredi. Quand viens–tu me rendre visite?
this   me   to visit

Maman: Oh mon Dieu, pas maintenant! Pas pendant l'hiver! Tu sais que je n'aime pas
not   during   know that

(vuh vuh-nee-rahN nay-tay)   *(fuh-rah sho)*
la neige. Je veux venir en été, quand il fera chaud.
it will be

Elise: D'accord. Oui, il fait trop froid ici en hiver.

Je reviendrai peut–être pour les vacances.
will go back perhaps

(kehl boh nee-day)   *(ruh-vyaN)*
Maman: Quelle bonne idée! Reviens à la maison, chérie.
what a   come back

(kohm)   *(luh seh)*   *(duh tahN zahN tahN)*
Comme tu le sais, il y a du soleil de temps en temps ici.
as   from time to time

Et pas de neige!

Elise: OK, maman. A bientôt.

Maman: Au revoir, ma chérie. Bon courage!
keep your chin up

PRACTICE

Comprenez-vous?
Do you understand?

See if you can answer the following questions based on the dialog.

(kee)
1. Qui a froid? _____
who

2. Où est Elise? _____

3. Où pleut-il? _____

4. Quand Elise travaille-t-elle? _____

See if you can match the numbers of each statement on the right to the appropriate picture of the person to make each statement true. The first one is done for you.

① Elle dit qu'il pleut.

② Elle a froid.

③ Elle travaille du lundi au samedi.

④ Elle dit qu'elle n'aime pas la neige.

⑤ Elle va travailler en avion et en voiture.

⑥ Elle veut aller en Alaska en été.

⑦ Elle reviendra à la maison en avion en décembre.

⑧ Elle aime travailler à Anchorage.

PRACTICE

Quel temps fait–il?
What's the weather?

Let's see if you can complete the sentences with the weather expressions given. (You can peak back at Chapter 7 to review *les mois et les saisons*.)

1. En été _____.
   it is hot

2. En avril _____.
   it rains a lot

3. En novembre _____.
   it's bad weather

4. En janvier _____.
   it snows

5. Au printemps _____.
   it is windy

6. En juillet _____.
   it's humid

7. Aujourd'hui _____.
   it's beautiful

EXPRESSIONS FOR TIME

You may recall the words *hier* (yesterday) and *aujourd'hui* (today) from Chapter 6 when you learned about giving directions. Now let's add *demain* (tomorrow) to your vocabulary. (Remember how *maman* described *le temps à Paris?*)

(yehr)
hier
yesterday

(oh-zhoor-dwee)
aujourd'hui
today

(duh-maN)
demain
tomorrow

Here are some useful time expressions:

(lah suh-mehn dehr-nyehr)
la semaine dernière
last week

(lah suh-mehn proh-shehn)
la semaine prochaine
next week

(ah-vahN tyehr)
avant–hier
the day before yesterday

(ah-preh duh-maN)
après demain
the day after tomorrow

PRACTICE AND REVIEW

See if you can figure out which word doesn't belong in each of the series of words below. Write the words in the blanks.

_____ 1. chaud, été, soleil, neige

_____ 2. hier, froid, demain, aujourd'hui

_____ 3. beaucoup, quand, où, qui

_____ 4. travaille, visite, ici, va

_____ 5. jour, semaine, année, printemps

(fehr)
FAIRE
to make/do

je fais	*(zhuh feh)*	*I make, do*
tu fais	*(tew feh)*	*you make, do*
il, elle, on fait	*(eel, ehl, ohN feh)*	*he, she, one makes*
nous faisons	*(noo fuh-zohN)*	*we make, do*
vous faites	*(voo feht)*	*you make, do*
ils, elles font	*(eel, ehl fohN)*	*they make, do*

CHAPTER 10

(voo-za-vay luhr, seel-voo-pleh)
Vous avez l'heure, s'il vous plaît?
Do you have the time, please?

You've learned *les jours de la semaine* (Chapter 5) *et les mois de l'année* (Chapter 7). Now it's time to learn about how to tell time. If you need to, go back to Chapters 2 and 4 to review *les nombres* up to 22. Later in this chapter you'll learn some more numbers that you'll need in order to say the minutes.

(ehtr duh boh new-muhr)
être de bonne humeur
to be in a good mood

(ehtr duh moh-veh-zew-muhr)
être de mauvaise humeur
to be in a bad mood

(eh-trahN nah-vahNs)
être en avance
to be early

(eh-trahN ruh-tahr)
être en retard
to be late

(lah gahr)
la gare
railroad station

(luh bee-yeh/leh bee-yeh)
le billet/les billets
ticket/tickets

(luh keh)
le quai
track

(lah gahr)
la gare
railroad station

(ewn mee-newt/deh mee-newt)
une minute/des minutes
minute/minutes

(zewt)
Zut!
Darn!

DIALOG

Antoine et Florence arrivent à la gare. Ils veulent prendre le train pour rendre visite à
want   to take   to visit

(luhr zah-mee nees)
leurs amis à Nice.
their

(seel voo pleh)   (poo-vay-voo meh)   (deer kahN pahr luh)
Antoine: S'il vous plaît, pouvez–vous me dire quand part le

(proh-shaN traN poo-uhr nees)
prochain train pour Nice?

Employé: Il part à 10:19.

(ko-mahN)   (ah keh luhr)
Antoine: Comment? A quelle heure?
at what

(muh-syuh)
Employé: 10:19, monsieur.

(eh-teel mahN-tnahN)
Antoine: Quelle heure est–il maintenant?
now

(voo zah-vey)   (mee-newt)
Employé: Il est 10:16. Vous avez trois minutes.
have

(dee)   (ee-lee-ya)   (dahN)
Antoine dit à Florence: Il y a un train dans trois minutes!
says   there is

(zewt pah duh shahNs ohN neh tahN ruh-tahr)
Florence: Zut! Pas de chance. On est en retard.
no luck   we

(seh too-zhoor)   (meh mee-stahwr)
Antoine: C'est toujours la même histoire.
always   same story

(noo sohm)   (ahN ruh tahr)
Nous sommes toujours en retard.
we   are

Florence: Tu es de mauvaise humeur
aujourd'hui, non?

(sa sew-fee)
Antonio: Ça suffit!
that's enough

Florence *(à l'employé)* : *(ah lahN-plwah-yay)* A quelle heure part le prochain train pour Nice? *(pahr luh proh-shaN traN poor nees)* Nous ne

pouvons pas attraper ce train. *(poo-vohN pah zah-trah-pay seh)*
can't catch   this

Employé: *(vwah-yohN)* Voyons......le prochain train pour Nice part à 13:47. *(pahr)*
let's see   leaves

(ruh-gahrd)
Florence regarde Antoine.

Antoine: *(seh kool)* C'est cool.

Florence *(à l'employé)*: *(sah mahrsh)* Ça marche.
that works

Deux billets, s'il vous plaît. *(duh bee-yeh)*

Employé: *(ah-lay saNpl oo ah-lay ruh-toor)* Aller simple ou aller–retour?
one-way   round-trip

Florence: Aller–retour, s'il vous plaît.

En deuxième classe. *(ahN duh-zyem klahs)*

Employé: *(sah feh)* Ça fait 30 euros. *(vwah-see voh)* Voici vos billets...
that makes   here are your

(ah-lohN-zee)
Allons–y!
Let's go!

Florence: *(kehl keh)* Merci. quel quai?
which

Employee: *(new-may-ro)* Le quai numéro 8. *(bohn vwah-yazh)* Bon voyage!
have a good trip

Antoine *(à Florence)* : *(byaN ah-lohr vuh tew prahN druhN vehr)* Bien...alors, veux–tu prendre un verre?...
good then   to have a drink

Florence: *(ah-vehk pleh-zeer seh ay-tohn-nahN)* Avec plaisir! C'est étonnant. *(eh duh boh new-muhr maN-tnahN)* Tu es de bonne humeur maintenant!
pleasure   amazing

Antoine: *(noo nuh sohm plew zahN)* Bien sûr. Nous ne sommes plus en retard maintenant. *(sohm zahN ah-vahNs)* Nous sommes en avance!
no longer

60

DO YOU UNDERSTAND?

Answer True or False to the following statements based on the dialog.

_____ 1. Antoine et Florence voyagent en avion.
plane

(duh-mahNd)
_____ 2. Antoine demande l'heure.
asks

(pahNs kuh)
_____ 3. Antoine pense que Florence est de mauvaise humeur.
thinks that

_____ 4. Florence demande trois billets.

_____ 5. Ils vont faire l'aller–retour.
to do

WHAT TIME IS IT?

(keh luh reh teel)
Quelle heure est–il?
What time is it? (This is another way to ask the time.)

Expressing time in French is simple. Just say the number of the hour
followed by the word *heure(s)*. If it's not clear from the context, you need
to state whether the time is *du matin* (AM), *de l'après-midi* (PM) for the
afternoon, or *du soir* (PM) for the evening.

In Europe as well as in French-speaking Canada, the 24-hour system of
telling time ("military" time as we call it in the U.S.) is usually used on TV
and radio, with travel schedules, appointments, and theater and concert
times in order to avoid ambiguity. Just subtract 12 to figure out the time you
are familiar with in the U.S. (16 hours is 16–12= 4 PM)

(eel eh seh tuhr)
Il est sept heures
du matin.

Il est midi.

(trwah-zuhr)
Il est trois heures
de l'après-midi.

(wee-tuhr)
Il est huit heures
du soir.

(dew mah-taN)
du matin
in the morning

(mee-dee)
midi
noon

(duh lah-preh-mee-dee)
de l'après-midi
in the afternoon

(dew swahr)
du soir
in the evening

Here are the ways to add the minutes when you are telling time:

(ohN zuhr)
Il est onze heures

(kah-rahNt)
quarante du matin.

(seh tuhr)
Il est sept heures

(vaN)
vingt du matin.

(trwah zuhr)
Il est trois heures

(mwaN dees)
moins dix de l'après-midi.
minus

(nuh vuhr)
Il est neuf heures

(ay duh-mee)
et demie du matin.
half

Note: *heures* is abbreviated to *h* when the time is written in numbers: 7h15 (or 19h15 using the 24–hour clock).

Other possibilities to say the time:

1. You can also say the time and add the minutes instead of saying the next hour *moins* (minus) the minutes: 2:50 is also: *(duh zuhr)*   *(sahN-kahNt)*
Il est deux heures cinquante.

2. For 8:15, you can use *et quart* (and a quarter) or use the number of minutes: *Il est huit heures quinze.*

3. For 8:45, you could say either:
Il est huit heures quarante-cinq or *Il est neuf heures moins le quart.*
(Notice with *moins* it is <u>*le quart*</u>, not <u>*et*</u> *quart*.)

4. For 9:30, you can use *et demie* (half) or use the number of minutes:
Il est neuf heures trente.

Match the times with the clocks. Write the correct letter under each clock.

a. Il est dix heures et quart.   b. Il est trois heures quarante-cinq.
c. Il est onze heures trente-huit.   d. Il est cinq heures et demie.
e. Il est huit heures cinquante.

1. _____   2. _____   3. _____   4. _____   5. _____

NUMBERS 23-100

You'll need to know higher *nombres* if you want to understand *les minutes* when someone tells you the time (...not to mention how important these numbers are for shopping or even revealing your age if the situation presents itself.) Read the pronunciation carefully and say each number out loud.

There are three things you should notice about these higher numbers that will help you memorize them.

1. Use *et* (and) only in the numbers 21, 31, 41, 51, 61, and 71. Use a hyphen in all others up to 99.

2. Don't use the word *un* (one) in 100 *(cent)* *(sahN)* or in 1000 *(mille)* *(meel)*.

3. The numbers from 70 to 100 involve doing some math. Look at these examples:

   70 = 60+10   81 = 4 x 20 + 1
   75 = 60+15   89 = 4 x 20 + 9
   80 = 4 x 20   90 = 80 + 10

In Switzerland and Belgium, however, the old forms of *septante (sehp-tahNt)* (70), sometimes *huitante (ew-ee-tahNt)* (80), and *nonante (nohnaNt)* (90) are used – and are easier to remember!

23	vingt-trois	*(vaN- trwah)*	40	quarante	*(kah-rahNt)*
24	vingt-quatre	*(vaN-kahtr)*	50	cinquante	*(saN-kahNt)*
25	vingt-cinq	*(vaN-saNk)*	60	soixante	*(swah-sahNt)*
26	vingt-six	*(vaN-sees)*	70	soixante-dix	*(swah-sahNt-dees)*
27	vingt-sept	*(vaN-seht)*	71	soixante et onze	*(swah-sahN-tay-ohNz)*
28	vingt-huit	*(vaN-weet)*	72	soixante-douze	*(swah-sahNt-dooz)*
29	vingt-neuf	*(vaN-nuhf)*	80	quatre-vingts	*(kahtr-vaN)*
30	trente	*(trahNt)*	85	quatre-vingt-cinq	*(kahtr-vaN-sahNk)*
31	trent-et-un	*(trahN-tay-uhN)*	90	quartre-vingt-dix	*(kahtr-vaN-dees)*
32	trente-deux	*(trahNt-duh)*	100	cent	*(sahN)*

CHAPTER 11

(kuh feh-tew pahN-dahN tohN tahN leebr)
Que fais–tu pendant ton temps libre?
What do you do in your free time?

(prohpr koh muhN soo nuhf)
propre comme un sou neuf
neat as a pin

(o puh-tee mah-taN)
au petit matin
at the crack of dawn

(uhN faN kew-ee-zee-nyay)
un fin cuisinier
a real gourmet cook

FOCUS: PREPOSITIONS

(dahN)
dans
in

(duh-vahN)
devant
in front of

(soo)
sous
under

(duh-dahN)
dedans
inside

(sewr)
sur
on

(deh-ryehr)
derrière
behind

(ahN dohr duh)
en dehors de
outside

(ah ko-tay duh)
à côté (de)
next to

USEFUL EXPRESSIONS

(vwah-lah)
voilà
there is/there are

(sewr-fay sewr luh wehb)
surfer sur le Web
surf the Web

(ahN-vwa-yay uhN ee-mehl)
envoyer un email
send email

VOCABULARY

(ahN bah)
en bas
downstairs

(ahN-o)
en haut
upstairs

(luh shyaN)
le chien
dog

(lay pehr-sohn)
les personnes
people

(zhuhn)
jeune
young

(lohr-dee-nah-tuhr)
l'ordinateur (m)
computer

(luh shah/lah shaht)
le chat(m)/la chatte (f)
cat

(vyuh)   (vyay)
vieux (m)/vieille (f)
old

STORY

(sah-mee eh-tuhN puh-tee shyaN mah-rohN) *(eelah-beet)*   *(ah-veh kewn shaht nwahr kee)*
Sami est un petit chien marron.   Il habite dans une maison avec une chatte noire qui
                                                live

   (mo-vehz) *(eelya)*   *(pehr-sohn kee ah-bee to-see)*   *(seht meh-zohN)*
s'appelle Mauvaise. Il y a trois personnes qui habitent aussi dans cette maison: une
                                                                    this

(fahm   uhN vyay-ohm)   *(uhN zhun gahr-sohN)*
femme, un vieil homme, et un jeune garçon.

Leur maison est propre comme un

            (rahN soo-vahN vee-zee ta)
sou neuf. Sami rend souvent visite à

(lewk   ahN-fahN)
Luc, un enfant de sept ans, dans sa chambre

            (ehm sahswahr)   *(lee)*
en haut. Sami aime s'asseoir sur le lit

(pahN-dahN kuh)   *(zhoo)*   *(seh zhoo-ay)*
pendant que Luc joue avec ses jouets.

(mo-vehz)   *(dohr)*
Mauvaise, la chatte, dort sous le lit.
                  sleeps (from dormir)

(to-mah)   *(pah-say dew)*
Thomas, le grand–père de Luc, aime passer du

(tahN dahN kwee-zeen) *(ah-dohr kwee-zee-nay)*
temps dans la cuisine. Il adore cuisiner.
                            to cook

                              (ah ko-tay dew foor)   *(puh ah-lohr sahN-teer)*
En fait, il est un fin cuisinier. Sami aime s'asseoir à côté du four. Il peut alors sentir de
                                                                  can   then smell

(day-lee-see-yuh zo-duhr)   *(kwee-zeen)*   *(tah-pee)*   *(fuh-nehtr)*
délicieuses odeurs quand Thomas cuisine. Mauvaise dort sur le tapis devant la fenêtre.
         smells   rug   window

      (fehr lah grahs mah-tee-nay)   *(kah-treen)*   *(suh lehv)*
Sami aime "faire la grasse matinée", mais Catherine, la mère de Luc, se lève au petit
              to sleep in   gets up

   (vah)   *(sohN bew-ro)* *(meh ahN root)* *(sohN nohr-dee-nah-tuhr)* *(lee say zee-mehl   sewrf)*
matin, va en bas à son bureau et met en route son ordinateur. Elle lit ses emails et surfe
     goes   office   boots up   reads

(dohr) *(kohr-beh yah pah-pyay)*

sur le Web. Mauvaise dort dans la corbeille à papier.
sleeps *wastepaper basket*

(o-see leer)

Catherine aime aussi lire des
to read

(ro-mahN trah-vah-yay) *(zhahr-dahN)*

romans et travailler dans son jardin
novels *work* *garden*

(tahN leebr)

dans son temps libre.
free time

(zhoo-ay dew pee-ah-no) *(suh kahsh)*

Luc aime jouer du piano. Sami se cache
to play piano *hides*

(kah-nah-pay) *(sah-lohN)*

derrière le canapé dans le salon quand Luc
sofa *livingroom*

(nehm pah brew-ee)

joue du piano. Mauvaise n'aime pas le bruit.
noise

(ah-lohr)

Alors, elle va dehors et dort dans le
so

(prehsk too lay vahN-druh-dee) *(vohN)* *(ruh-gahr-day)*

jardin. Presque tous les vendredis, Thomas, Catherine et Luc vont en haut regarder la
almost every Friday *go* *watch*

(tay-lay) *(leevr oo)* *(o kahrt)* *(sahl duh zhuh)*

télé, lire des livres, ou jouer aux cartes dans la salle de jeux. Mauvaise dort sur la
TV *read books* *or* *cards* *game room*

(shehz) *(sah-syay)* *(preh)*

chaise et Sami s'assied par terre près de sa famille.
sits *near*

(ah ewn vee ah-say kohN-fohr-tahbl)

Sami a une vie assez confortable.
life *quite*

DO YOU UNDERSTAND?

(keh skeel-zehm fehr)
Qu'est-ce qu'ils aiment faire? (What do they like to do?) Match the members of the family with the things they like to do. Write the letters in the blanks.

1. Sami aime _____   A. jouer du piano

2. Mauvaise aime _____   B. cuisiner

3. Catherine aime _____   C. dormir

4. Thomas aime _____   D. rendre visite à la salle de Luc

5. Luc aime _____   E. surfer sur le Web

(eh-may)
AIMER
to like, to love

Aimer is a common French verb that is used for people and things that you like or love. *Adorer* is another verb you can use when you want to say you love or adore someone or something. *Je t'aime (zhuh tehm)* and *Je t'adore (zhuh tah-dohr)* both mean "I love you".

j'aime	*(zhehm)*	*I like, love*
tu aimes	*(tew ehm)*	*you like, love*
il, elle, on aime	*(eel, ehl, ohN ehm)*	*he, she, one likes, loves*
nous aimons	*(noo zehmohN)*	*we like, love*
vous aimez	*(voo zehmay)*	*you like, love*
ils, elles aiment	*(eel, ehl zehm)*	*they like, love*

68

PRACTICE

Use the picture below to help you fill in the blanks with *dans, sur, sous, à côté de ou derrière*.

1. L'homme est _____ le lit.

2. Il y a une chatte _____ le lit.
   there is

3. Le lit est _____ le tapis.

4. La fenêtre est _____ le lit.

5. Il y a des jouets _____ le lit.

6. Il y a une corbeille à papier _____ du lit.

Now write 2 sentences of your own describing the picture.

1. _____

2. _____

CHAPTER 12

(ah-tew pah-say uhN bohN wee-kend)
As–tu passé un bon week end?
Did you have a good weekend?

(seh luhN-dee mah-tahN vaN-sahN ay mohN-neek sohN to tra-vahy)
C'est lundi matin. Vincent et Monique sont au travail.
are   at   work

Vincent: Bonjour, Monique. As–tu passé un bon week end?

(say-teh zhay-nyahl)
Monique: Bonjour, Vincent. Oui, c'était génial.
it was great

(keh-skuh tew ah feh)
Vincent: Ah bon? Qu'est–ce que tu as fait?
really   what did you do

(zhay zhoo-ay o teh-nees)
Monique: Samedi j'ai joué au tennis.

(swee zah-lay vwahr uhN kohN-sehr)
Samedi soir je suis allée voir un concert
I went   to see

(sew-pehr)
des Rolling Stones. C'était super!

(luhr mew-zeek)
Vincent: J'adore leur musique.

(frahNsh-mahN)
Franchement, je suis surpris
frankly

(keel   zhoo ahN-kohr)
qu'ils jouent encore.
that   are still playing

Monique: Qu'est–ce que tu as fait ce week end? As-tu joué au foot comme d'habitude?
(o foot kohm dah-bee-tewd)
did you play soccer as usual

Vincent: Oui, j'ai joué au foot *(zhay joo-ay)* samedi et hier soir *(yehr swahr)* j'ai regardé un film *(feelm)* avec mon neveu. *(nuh-vuh)*
I played *nephew*

Monique: Quel film, *(kehl)* avez-vous vu? *(ah-vay voo vew)*
did you see

Vincent: On a vu le nouveau film *(ohN nah vew noo-vo)* de Harry Potter. *(ah-ree po-tehr)*
new

Monique: Oh! Il est bien?

Vincent: Oui, J'ai pensé que c'était très amusant, *(zhay pahN-say say-teh treh zah-mew-zahN)*

mais mon neveu a eu un peu peur. *(ah ew uhN puh puhr)*
was a little afraid

Monique: Ma fille veut le voir, *(fee-y)* mais moi, *(mwah)*
it

je préfère les films romantiques. *(ro-mahN-teek)*

Vincent: Oh, vraiment? *(vreh-mahN mwah-o-see)* Moi aussi.
really me too

Monique: Allez, tu blagues! *(blahg)*
come on you're joking

Vincent: Non, je ne blague pas!

On se verra à la réunion ce matin. *(ohN suh vehr-rah) (ray-ew-nyohN)*
we'll see each other at the meeting

Monique: Zut! Quelle réunion? *(zewt kehl)*
darn what

MATCHING

Match the questions and statements on the left with the appropriate responses on the right.

_____ 1. Qu'est-ce que tu as fait ce week end?   a) Oui, j'ai passé un bon week end.

_____ 2. As-tu passé un bon week end?   b) Quel film as-tu vu?

_____ 3. J'ai vu un film hier soir.   c) J'ai joué au foot.

_____ 4. Comment était le concert?   d) Oui.
               how

_____ 5. Tu blagues!   e) C'était génial!

_____ 6. Il est bien?   f) Non! Je ne blague pas.

SIMPLE PAST TENSE VERBS

There are several past tenses in French, as there are in English. The passé composé *(pah-say kohN-po-zay)* is most commonly used as the past tense in French. It is a compound tense, which means it is made up of two parts: a helping verb *avoir (ah-vwahr)* (have) or *être (ehtr)* (be) and a past participle *J'ai <u>vu</u> (zhay vew)* (I saw), *J'ai <u>pensé</u> (zhay pahN-say)* (I thought), *Je suis <u>allé</u> (zhuh swee zah-lay)* (I went).

Most of the time in American English we don't use the helping verb. Instead of "I have eaten" we would say in English "I ate." The helping verb ("have"–*ai*– in this case) must be used in French: *J'ai mangé (zhay mahN-zhay)* ("I ate.").

To form the *passé composé* use the present tense of the helping verb plus a past participle. For verbs that end in -er in infinitive form (like *penser - pahN-say* - to think), just take off the -er from the verb *(pens)* and add -é *(pensé)*.

(pahN-say)
PENSER (passé composé)
to think

J'ai pensé	*(zhay pahN-say)*	*I thought*
Tu as pensé	*(tew ah pahN-say)*	*you thought*
Il, elle, on a pensé	*(eel, ehl, ohN (n)ah pahN-say)*	*he, she, one thought*
Nous avons pensé	*(noo zahvohN pahN-say)*	*we thought*
Vous avez pensé	*(voo zahvay pahN-say)*	*you thought*
Ils, elles ont pensé	*(eel, ehl zohN pahN-say)*	*they thought*

Some verbs use *être* (to be) to form the *passé composé*. Many words that express motion are used with *être*, like *aller* (to go), *arriver* (to arrive), and *venir* (to come). In the dialog in this chapter Monique said, *Je suis allée.* (I went.)

Notice that if you are writing, the past participle must agree with the subject. If the subject is feminine like Monique add an –e (*Je suis allée.*) If the subject is plural, add an –s *Nous sommes allés.* (We went.) If "we" refers to women and/or girls only, then it would be *Nous sommes allées.* (with that extra "e".)

So, the past participles of *être* act a little like adjectives since they agree in number and gender: For example:

MASCULINE SINGULAR   il est allé

FEMININE SINGULAR   elle est allée

MASCULINE PLURAL   ils sont allés

FEMININE PLURAL   elles sont allées

If this sounds confusing, the good news is that when you *say* the following forms of *aller*, they have exactly the same pronunciation: *aller, allé, allée, allés, allées (ah-lay).*

<table>
<tr><td colspan="3" align="center">(ah-lay)
A L L E R (passé composé)
to go</td></tr>
<tr><td colspan="3" align="center">masculine forms</td></tr>
<tr><td>Je suis allé</td><td>(zhuh swee zah-lay)</td><td>I went</td></tr>
<tr><td>Tu es allé</td><td>(tew eh zah-lay)</td><td>you went</td></tr>
<tr><td>Il est allé</td><td>(eel, eh tah-lay)</td><td>he went</td></tr>
<tr><td>Nous sommes allés</td><td>(noo sohm zah-lay)</td><td>we went</td></tr>
<tr><td>Vous êtes allés</td><td>(voo zeh tah-lay)</td><td>you went</td></tr>
<tr><td>Ils sont allés</td><td>(eel sohN tah-lay)</td><td>they went</td></tr>
</table>

PRACTICE

Use the pictures to help you fill in the blanks with the passé composé. Choose a past participle verb from the list and **add the helping verb**. Remember to use the present tense of **avoir** (have) or **être** (be), then the past participle. Examples: **J'ai mangé.** ("I ate.") **Il est allé.** (He went.)

Choose one of these words to complete your passé composé verbs.

nagé	allé	mangé	téléphoné
regardé	joué	parlé	pensé

Hier, j' _____ à mon amie.

            1.

Nous _____ beaucoup du week end.

      2.

Elle était très fatiguée samedi parce

qu'elle _____ au foot toute la matinée.
                    3.

(reh-stay zheh zehl)
Alors, elle est restée chez elle le dimanche
         stayed   at home

et _____ la télé toute la journée.
            4.

Puis, elle m'a demandé "Qu'est–ce que tu as fait?" Je lui ai dit

                                                            (lahk)
que le samedi mon petit ami et moi _____ dans le lac.
                            5. *(Just guess!)*   *lake*

                                                            (boom)
Samedi soir nous _____ à une boum.
                        6.   *party*

CHAPTER 13

(kehs kuh tew vuh mahN-zhay)
Qu'est–ce que tu veux manger?
What do you want to eat?

zhay ewn faN duh loo
J'ai une faim de loup
I'm as hungry as a horse.

ah vohtr sahN-tay
A votre santé!
Cheers!

bohN ah-pay-tee
Bon appétit!
Have a good meal!

VOCABULARY

(luh tay)
le thé
tea

(luh leh)
le lait
milk

(luh kah-fay)
le café
coffee

(luh vaN)
le vin
wine

(lah bee-yehr)
la bière
beer

(lay frew-ee)
les fruits(m)
fruit

(lah-nah-nah)
l'ananas (m)
pineapple

(lah suh-reez)
la cerise
cherry

(luh day-sehr)
le dessert
dessert

(luh gah-to)
le gâteau
cake

(lah pohm)
la pomme
apple

(la frehz)
la fraise
strawberry

(loh-nyohN)
l'oignon
onion

(lah glahs)
la glace
ice cream

(lah tahrt)
la tarte
pie

(lah bah-nahn)
la banane
banana

(luh paN)
le pain
bread

(luh ree)
le riz
rice

(loh-rahNzh)
l'orange (f)
orange

(lay freet)
les frites
French fries

(lah vee-ahNd)
la viande
meat

(luh poo-leh)
le poulet
chicken

(lah kah-roht)
la carotte
carrot

(luh buhf)
le boeuf
beef

(luh shahN-pee-nyohN)
le champignon
mushroom

(luh jahN-bohN)
le jambon
ham

(lah toh-maht)
la tomate
tomato

(lah soop)
la soupe
soup

(luh froh-mazh)
le fromage
cheese

(lay lay-gewm)
les légumes
vegetables

(lah sah-lahd)
la salade
salad

STORY

(trwah zah-mee sohN dahN zuhN reh-stoh-rahN) (ahN-ree, greh-gwahr, ay-reek)
Trois amis sont dans un restaurant: Henri, Grégoire, Eric

       (keh-skuh)   *(voo voo-lay mahN-zhay)*
Henri: Qu'est–ce que vous voulez manger?
What do you want to eat?

        (nay pah)   *(soop)*   *(sah-lahd)*
Grégoire: Je n'ai pas très faim. Je prends une soupe et une salade.

       (twah)
Henri: Et toi, Eric?

                     (mahN-zhay)   *(suh mah-taN)*
Eric: Moi? J'ai une faim de loup. Je n'ai pas mangé de petit déjeuner ce matin.
                                        this morning

(sehr-vuhr) (keh-skuh)   *(voo day-zee-ray)*
Le serveur: Qu'est–ce que vous désirez?

       (zhuh prahN)   *(ewn sah-land vehrt)*
Grégoire: Je prends de la soupe et une salade verte.

      (bohN) (poor)   *(muh-syuh)*
Le serveur: Bon. Pour vous, monsieur?

           (ew noh-mleh to froh-mazh)
Henri: Moi, je voudrais une omelette au fromage et une salade de tomates.

      (kwa dotr)
Le serveur: Quoi d'autre?
      something else

(kohm deh-sehr)
Henri: Oui. S'il vous plaît, comme dessert je voudrais de la tarte aux pommes.

(ay voo)
Le serveur: Et vous, monsieur?

(dah-bohrd)   *(day zehs-kahr-go)*   *(ahN-treh)*   *(dew poo-lay)* *(moo-tahrd)*
Eric: D'abord, je voudrais des escargots en entrée. Ensuite...du poulet à la moutarde.

(krehm kah-rah-mehl)
Comme dessert, je prends de la crème caramel, s'il vous plaît.

(zhuh swee) (day-zo-lay)   *(noo nah-vohN plew)*
Le serveur: Je suis désolé, monsieur. Nous n'avons plus de poulet. Nous avons un très
        am   sorry   have no more

(so-mohN sehr-vee ah-veh-kewn so so see-trohN)
bon saumon servi avec une sauce au citron.
        salmon   lemon

(dah-kohr)   *(voo voo-lay uhN day-sehr)*
Eric: D'accord. Je prends le saumon.   **Le Serveur:** Vous voulez un dessert?

(glah sah lah vah-nee-y)   *(bwa-sohN)*
Eric: Oui. Je voudrais de la glace à la vanille.   **Le Serveur:** Comme boisson?
                                                                drink

(kah-rahf duh blahN)
Henri: Nous prenons une carafe de blanc, s'il vous plaît.
        a carafe of white wine

(ehk-say-lahN)
Le Serveur: Excellent.

Henri, Grégoire, et Eric: A votre santé! Bon appétit!

PRACTICE

FOOD VOCABULARY

Use the clues in English to find the words *en français*.

ACROSS

3. cake
5. wine
7. cheese
8. fish

Down

1. mushroom
2. ham
4. ice cream
6. milk
7. strawberry

REVIEW

(vreh oo fo)
Comprenez–vous?: Vrai ou faux
true or false

1. Eric a très faim. _____

2. La tarte à la pomme est un dessert. _____

3. Henri a commandé du vin rouge. _____

4. Eric mange du poulet. _____

5. Eric veut de la glace au chocolat. _____

FOCUS: GRAMMAR

SOME, ANY

When speaking about food, you will want to use "some". You say *J'aime __la glace__* (I like ice cream), but *Je voudrais __de la glace__* (I would like some ice cream.) See the chart below to see the different forms of "some" that you use before the noun.

de + le = du *(dew)*	du fromage *(dew froh-mazh)*	some cheese
de + la = de la *(duh lah)*	de la salade *(duh lah sah-lahd)*	some salad
de + les = des *(day)*	des fraises *(day frehz)*	some strawberries
de + l' = de l' *(duhl)*	de l'eau *(duh lo)*	some water

If you want to say that you DON'T want something, just use *de* (which means "any" in a negative sentence). *Je ne veux pas __de__ dessert*. (I don't want any dessert.)

CHAPTER 14

(keh-skuh tew ah)
Qu'est–ce que tu as?
What's the matter? What's wrong?

(zhuh swee kruh-vay)
Je suis crevée
I'm exhausted.

(zhwah-yuh zah-nee-vehr-sehr)
Joyeux anniversaire!
Happy Birthday!

(keh-skuh tew ah)
Qu'est–ce que tu as?
What's the matter?

(zhuh muh sahN mahl)
Je me sens mal.
I feel sick.

VOCABULARY

(feh-tay)	*(uhN rewm)*	*(mah-lahd)*	*(lah sahN-tay)*
fêter	un rhume	malade	la santé
to celebrate	*a cold*	*sick/ill*	*health*
(pwah)	*(uhN vay-lo)*	*(luh zhahr-daN)*	*(uhN vehr)*
poids	un vélo	le jardin	un verre
weight	*a bicycle*	*the garden*	*a glass*

DIALOG

(trwah zah-mee suh ruh-troov   sheh)
Trois amies se retrouvent chez Sarah pour déjeuner et fêter l'anniversaire de Christine.
      meet   at the home of

Sarah: Salut, Christine! Joyeux anniversaire!

                    (kehl)   (mah-nyee-feek)   (ohN)   (dohr)
Christine: Salut, Sarah! Merci! Quel jour magnifique, aujourd'hui! On va déjeuner dehors?
                                                              we   outside

Sarah: Oui, dans le jardin...Julie, qu'est-ce que tu as?

Julie: Je me sens mal.

      (kehl doh-mazh)
Sarah: Quel dommage! As-tu un rhume?
      too bad

      (zhuh pahNs kuh wee)
Julie: Je pense que oui. J'ai mal à la
      I think so

      gorge et je suis crevée.

      (duh-pew-ee ko-byaN duh tahN eh-tew mah-lahd)
Sarah: Depuis combien de temps es-tu malade?
      how long have you been sick

            (ahN-vee-rohN)
Julie: Depuis environ deux jours.
      for about

      (poor-kwah eh-tew vuh-new)
Sarah: Pourquoi es-tu venue?
      why   did you come

                              (pahr-tee-see-pay)
Julie: C'est l'anniversaire de Christine! Je veux participer à la fête!

      (seh see zhahN-tee)   (pahr)
Christine: C'est si gentil de ta part, Julie. Merci.
      so nice of you

Julie: *(dah-yehr)* D'ailleurs, comment vas–tu, Christine? Tu étais si malade le mois dernier. *(mwah dehr-nyay)*
anyway   last month

Christine: *(veh) (maN-tnahN) (ruh-gahrd mwah) (pree uhN puh duh pwah)* Je vais bien maintenant. Regarde–moi! J'ai pris un peu de poids.
now   look   gained a little weight

Julie: *(seh fahN-tah-steek) (leh rahN plehn fohrm) (ko-mahN)* C'est fantastique. Tu as l'air en pleine forme! Comment va ton travail?
you look great

Christine: *(day-bohr-day)* Je suis débordée, mais c'est très intéressant.
swamped

(rahN-kohNtr shahk) (zhahN) (dee-fay-rahN) Je rencontre chaque jour des gens différents.
meet   people

Julie: *(shweht)* Chouette!
great

Sarah: *(ah tahbl)* A table! On va manger de la salade niçoise, de l'ananas, du pain, du
to the table *(nee-swahz)*
we are going to eat

(o shoh-co-lah kohm) *(koh-mahN-sohN)* *(vehr shahN-pah- nyuh)*
fromage, et un gâteau au chocolat comme dessert. Commençons avec un verre de champagne.
glass

J,C,S: *(ah vohtr sahN-tay)* A votre santé!
to your health (cheers)

Julie et Sarah: *(kah-rahN-tyehm)* Au quarantième anniversaire de Christine!

Christine: *(sewr-too)* Et à la santé surtout de Julie!
especially

Julie: *(day-zhah mee-yuh)* Je me sens déjà mieux!
I feel better already!

OUI OU NON?

Read *en anglais*. Answer *en français*.

_____ 1. Does Julie have a sore throat?

_____ 2. Does Christine like her job?

_____ 3. Is the celebration at Julie's house?

_____ 4. Is it Christine's thirtieth birthday?

_____ 5. Was Christine sick last month?

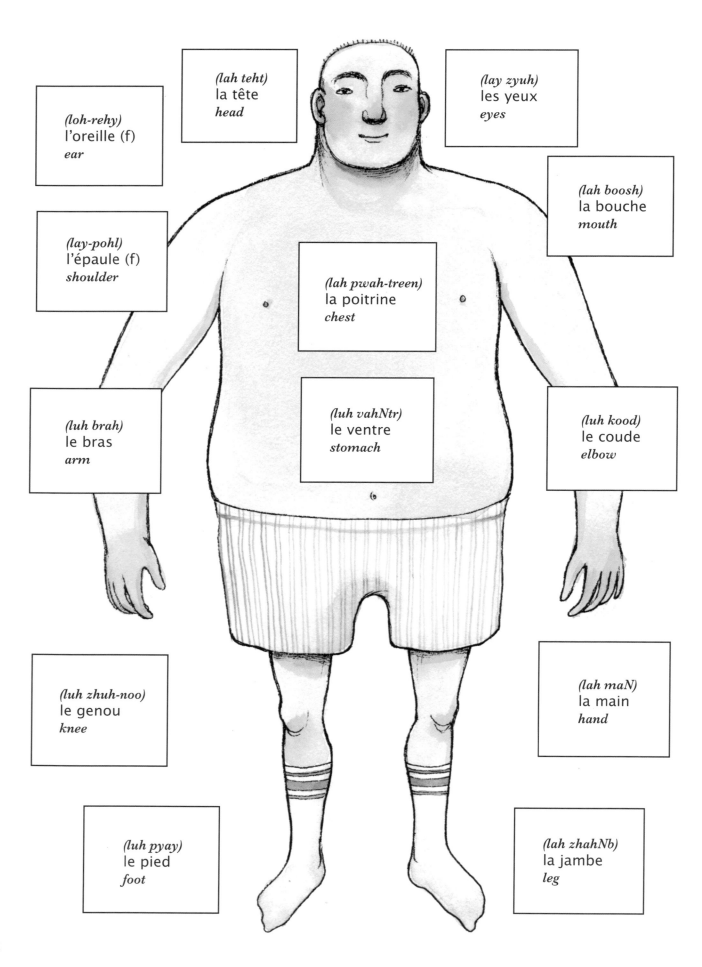

(loh-rehy)
l'oreille (f)
ear

(lah teht)
la tête
head

(lay zyuh)
les yeux
eyes

(lah boosh)
la bouche
mouth

(lay-pohl)
l'épaule (f)
shoulder

(lah pwah-treen)
la poitrine
chest

(luh brah)
le bras
arm

(luh vahNtr)
le ventre
stomach

(luh kood)
le coude
elbow

(luh zhuh-noo)
le genou
knee

(lah maN)
la main
hand

(luh pyay)
le pied
foot

(lah zhahNb)
la jambe
leg

PRACTICE

(keh-skuh voo zah-vay)
Qu'est–ce que vous avez?
What's the matter? (formal)

If you happen to get hurt or sick while you're in a French–speaking country, here's how you can tell someone what hurts or bothers you: use *avoir mal à* + the definite article+ the body part = *J'ai mal aux dents.* (My teeth hurt.)

Remember that Julie said, *"J'ai mal à la gorge."* (I have a sore throat.) See if you can match *l'anglais with le français* by looking at the diagram. Write the letters in the blanks.

1. J'ai mal au ventre. _____   a. My feet hurt.

2. J'ai mal au genou. _____   b. My eyes hurt.

3. J'ai mal à la tête. _____   c. I have a stomachache.

4. J'ai mal aux pieds. _____   d. My back hurts.

5. J'ai mal à l'oreille. _____   e. My neck hurts.

6. J'ai mal aux yeux. _____   f. My knee hurts.

7. J'ai mal au cou. _____   g. I have a headache.

8. J'ai mal au dos. _____   h. I have an earache.

You may remember that in Chapter 11 Sami *le chien* can *sentir* the good food in the oven. *Sentir* means "to smell", but when this verb becomes reflexive *(se sentir)*, it means "to feel". Reflexive just means that you perform an action upon yourself. You can recognize a reflexive verb by the reflexive pronouns that come right before the verb (unlike in English where the reflexive pronoun comes <u>after</u> the verb– I wash <u>myself</u>.)

You've seen this type of verb already with *Je m'appelle*... (My name is....) Literally it means "I call myself". *Je me brosse les dents (zhuh muh brohs lay dahN)* means "I brush my teeth." *Je me sens bien (zhuh muh sahN byaN)* = I feel good. *Je me sens mal* = I feel bad (sick).

(suh sahN-teer)
SE SENTIR
to feel

je me sens	*(zhuh muh sahN)*	*I feel*
tu te sens	*(tew tuh sahN)*	*you feel*
il, elle, on se sent	*(eel, ehl, ohN suh sahN)*	*he, she, one feels*
nous nous sentons	*(noo noo sahN-tohN)*	*we feel*
vous vous sentez	*(voo voo sahN-tay)*	*you feel*
ils, elles se sentent	*(eel, ehl suh sahNt)*	*they feel*

CHAPTER 15

(sah tuh vah ah mehr-vay-y)
Ça te va à merveille!
That looks great on you!

(zhah-meh duh lah vee)
Jamais de la vie!
No way!

(nuh tahN feh pah)
Ne t'en fais pas.
Don't worry.

(ahN sohld)
en solde
on sale

VOCABULARY

(luh mah-yo duh baN)
le maillot de bain
swimsuit

(luh kohs-tewm)
le costume
suit

(lay sho-seht)
les chaussettes(f)
socks

(luh pewl)
le pull
pullover

(lay-shahrp)
l'écharpe(f)
scarf (long)

(luh zheen)
le jean
jeans

(lah rohb)
la robe
dress

(luh koh-lahN)
le collant
tights

(luh shohrt)
le short
shorts

(luh foo-lahr)
le foulard
scarf

(luh shah-po)
le chapeau
hat

(lah vehst)
la veste
jacket

(laN-pehr-may-ahbl)
l'imperméable(m)
raincoat

(lah shuh-meez)
la chemise
shirt

(luh shuh-meez-yay)
le chemisier
blouse

(lah krah-vaht)
la cravate
tie

(lah saN-tewr)
la ceinture
belt

(luh pah-rah-plew-ee)
le parapluie
umbrella

(lah jewp)
la jupe
skirt

(luh pahN-tah-lohN)
le pantalon
pants

(lay boht)
les bottes (f)
boots

(lay sho-sewr)
les chaussures(f)
shoes

89

DIALOG

(mee-shehl ay mah-ree mahr-taN pahrt ahN vwah-yazh dah-fehr ah ah-wa-yi)   *(traN dahsh-tay)*
Michel et Marie Martin partent en voyage d'affaires à Hawaï. Ils sont en train d'acheter
            are leaving   *business trip*   *in the process of buying*

(day veht-mahN)   *(mahn-tnahN)*   *(mah-gah-zaN)*   *(poo rohm)*
des vêtements. Ils sont maintenant dans un magasin de vêtements pour hommes.
  clothes   *now*   *store*

      (eh-say)   *(gree)*
Michel essaie un costume gris.
      is trying on

              (suh)   *(tuh vah byaN)*   *(zhuh nuh veh pah zahN-pohr-tay)*
Marie: Ce costume te va bien, mais je ne vais pas emporter un costume.
        this   *fits you well*   *bring*

          (tew ah puh teht reh-zohN)   *(troh pa-bee-yay)*   *(day ray-ewnyohN ah ah-wa-yi)*
Michel: Tu as peut–être raison. C'est trop habillé pour des réunions à Hawaï.
          perhaps you're right   *It's too dressy for   meetings*

          (meh suh pahN-tah-lohn ay seht)
Marie: Mets ce pantalon et cette chemise rose.
        put on these pants   this

Michel: Rose? Jamais de la vie!

(dohn)
Donne–moi une chemise bleue, s'il te plaît.
give

          (pwee-zhuh voo zay-day)
Vendeur: Puis–je vous aider?
          can I help you

Michel: Avez–vous cette chemise en bleu?

          (mehm tah-y)
Vendeur: La même taille?
          the same size

Michel: Oui.

          (lah vwa-see)
Vendeur: La voici.
          here it is

Michel: *(seh myuh)* *(shehrsh o-see)* *(ewn vehs duh spohr)*
C'est mieux. Je cherche aussi une veste de sport.
that's better   am looking for   sport jacket

Vendeur: *(sehl-see eh tahN)*
Celle-ci est en solde.
this one

Marie: *(seh treh zay-lay-gahN)* *(sa tuh vah sew-pehr byaN shay-ree)*
C'est très élégant. Ça te va super bien, Chéri!
that fits you really well, dear

Michel: *(byaN zhah-sheht)*
Bien. J'achète le pantalon, la chemise et la veste.

Vendeur: *(pay-yay)* *(kehs lah-bah)*
Merci de payer à la caisse là-bas.
at cash register over there

Michel et Marie sont maintenant dans un magasin de vêtements pour femmes. Marie essaie une robe jaune.

Michel: *(zhoh-lee)* *(troh lohNg)*
Cette robe est jolie, mais elle est trop longue.
pretty   too   long

Marie: *(ahN deh-soo)*
Peut-être... Mademoiselle, avez-vous la taille en dessous pour cette robe?
a size smaller

Vendeuse: Non, madame, nous n'avons pas cette taille.

Michel: Regarde cette robe rouge, Chérie.

Marie: Cette robe est laide. Je ne peux pas mettre ça.
(lehd) *(nuh puh pah mehtr sa)*
ugly *I can't put that on*

Michel: Ne t'en fais pas. Je ne l'aime pas non plus!
it *either*

Vendeuse: Est–ce que cette jupe vous plaît, madame? C'est la dernière et elle est à votre taille.
(eh skuh) *(seht)* *(pleh)* *(dehr-nee-ehr)*
please you *last one* *your size*

Marie: Cette jupe me plaît beaucoup! **Michel:** Essaie–la!
(seht) *(muh)* *(eh-say lah)*
me

Vendeuse: Voici un chemisier jaune et une écharpe de soie à mettre avec la jupe.
(swah ah meh trah-vek)
silk *to put on with*

Marie: OK....Qu'est–ce que tu en penses? **Michel:** Ça te va à merveille!
(keh-skuh tew ahN pahNs)

Marie: Parfait! Allons voir les maillots de bains. Ensuite, nous serons prêts pour Hawaï.
(pahr-feh) *(ahN-sweet)* *(seh-rohN preh)*
let's go see *then* *we'll be ready*

DO YOU UNDERSTAND?

Which of these statements describe the situations in the dialogs? Put a check next to the sentences that are true.

1. _____ Michel achète une chemise rose.

2. _____ Marie aime la jupe.

3. _____ Michel essaie un imperméable.

4. _____ Michel et Marie vont à Hawaï.

Each of the 5 words below is a scrambled word for a piece of women's clothing. Unscramble each of the clue words. Copy the letters in the numbered cells to other cells with the same number. Then you will find the answer to the question! (The answer does not refer to the dialogs in this chapter. This is just to practice some of the new words you learned.)

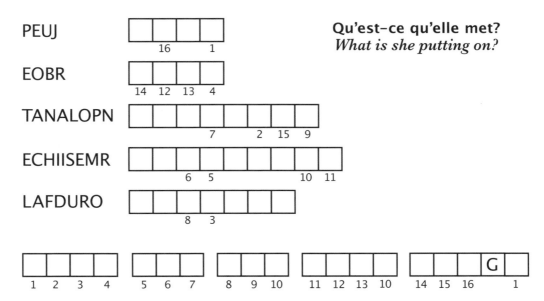

PEUJ

| | | 16 | | | 1 |

EOBR

| 14 | 12 | 13 | 4 |

TANALOPN

| | | | 7 | | 2 | 15 | 9 |

ECHIISEMR

| | | 6 | 5 | | | 10 | 11 |

LAFDURO

| | | 8 | 3 | | |

Qu'est-ce qu'elle met?
What is she putting on?

| 1 | 2 | 3 | 4 | | 5 | 6 | 7 | | 8 | 9 | 10 | | 11 | 12 | 13 | 10 | | 14 | 15 | 16 | G | 1 |

You saw some ways to say "this" in the dialog: <u>*ce costume*</u>, <u>*ce pantalon*</u>, <u>*cette*</u> *robe*, <u>*cette jupe*</u>. These are adjectives (demonstrative adjectives) so they must agree in gender and number with the noun they modify:

	SINGULAR			PLURAL		
Masculine	ce/cet* (suh/seht)	this/that		ces	(say)	these/those
Feminine	cette (seht)	this/that		ces	(say)	these/those

FOCUS

THIS, THAT, THESE, THOSE

In the dialog, you also saw *celle-ci (sehl-see)* which means "this one". "That one" in this case would be *celle-là (sehl-lah)*. These are forms of demonstrative pronouns that must also agree in gender and number with the nouns they refer to. (Notice that French demonstrative pronouns are different from demonstrative adjectives, unlike English.) Take a look at the chart:

	SINGULAR		PLURAL	
	this one	that one	these ones	those ones
Masculine	celui (suhlwee)-ci	celui-là	ceux (suh)-ci	ceux-là
Feminine	celle (sehl)-ci	celle-là	celles (sehl)-ci	celles-là

(seh-taN-pehr-may-ahbl)
*Use this in front of a masculine noun that starts with a vowel: *cet impermeable*

CHAPTER 16

(seh lah vee)
C'est la vie!
That's life!

No matter how much *vous* prepare for *un voyage* to a foreign country, there will often be some unexpected things that can happen. When some of these things are unfortunate or unpleasant, it helps to know some of *la langue* in order *comprendre* what people (like *les docteurs* or *les agents de police*) are asking. *Vous* might *aussi* need *expliquer* what happened. A good attitude goes a long way in preparing *vous* to cope with unfortunate circumstances. Accepting an unforeseen event as part of *votre* experience will help you get through it. You will see in the story in this chapter how Robert, from New York, handles *ses problèmes* on a business trip to Marseilles.

(kehl oh-ruhr)
Quelle horreur!
What a terrible thing!

(myuh vo tahr kuh zhah-meh)
Mieux vaut tard que jamais!
Better late than never!

VOCABULARY

(lay-krahN)
l'écran
screen

(luh pohr-tabl)
le portable (m)
laptop computer

(laN-pree-mahNt)
l'imprimante
printer

(luh ray-pohN-duhr)
le répondeur
answering machine

(lohr-dee-nah-tuhr)
l'ordinateur (m)
computer

(luh fahks)
le fax
fax machine

(luh tay-lay-fohn pohr-tahbl)
(le téléphone) portable
cell phone

(luh klah-vyay)
le clavier
keyboard

(lah soo-ree)
la souris
mouse

(suh kee eh tah-ree-vay)   *(vwah-yah zhah mahr-say-y)*
Read *ce qui est arrivé* to Robert on a *voyage à Marseilles*.
    what happened

                        (shahNs)   *(dah-fehr)*
Mon frère Robert n'a pas de chance.   Il est allé en voyage d'affaires à Marseille le mois
              is not lucky   *went*   *business trip*

                                       (voh-lay)   *(lah-ay-ro-pohr)*
dernier. D'abord, son ordinateur portable a été volé dans l'aéroport. Quelle horreur!
                              was stolen   *airport*

(ahNsweet)   *(eh-say-yay dahN-vwah-yay)*   *(bew-ro)*   *(pah-trohN)*
Ensuite, il a essayé d'envoyer un fax à son bureau de New York, mais son patron ne l'a
         tried to send   *office*   *his*   *boss*   *it*

    (reh-sew)   *(suh-lah)*   *(ew-tee-lee-zay)*   *(leh-say)*   *(meh-sahzh)*
pas reçu. Après cela, Robert a utilisé son téléphone portable pour laisser un message sur
         that   *used*   *leave*

                    (mahr-sheh)
le répondeur du travail, mais il ne marchait pas. Quelle horreur!
                wasn't working

    (swee-vahN)   *(eh tah-ree-vay)*   *(treh zay-nehr-vay)*
Le jour suivant, il est arrivé à Marseille. Robert était très énervé parce qu'il s'était
     following   *annoyed*   *because*

(pehr-dew)   *(rahN-day-voo)*
perdu et était en retard de 40 minutes sur son premier rendez–vous.
lost   *meeting*

     (kehl-kaN)   *(sahl lew-ee ah dee)*
(Quand quelqu'un dans la salle lui a dit "Mieux vaut tard que jamais!" D'abord il n'a
 when someone   *room*   *said to him*

    (kohN-pree luh sahNs)   *(ah-preh zah-vwahr)*   *(seh sahN-tee)*
pas compris le sens. Après avoir compris, il s'est senti un peu mieux.)
didn't understand the meaning   *after having*   *felt*   *better*

(ray-ew-see ah ahN-vwah-yay say zee-mehl)   *(kehl-kuh zah-mee)*

Robert a réussi à envoyer ses emails à son patron, sa famille, et à quelques amis. Il a
     succeeded   *some*

(troo-vay)   *(aN-tehr-neht)*   *(ew-tee-leez luhr zohr-dee-nah-tuhr) (prehsk)*

trouvé un café Internet pas loin de son hôtel. Il utilise leurs ordinateurs presque chaque
found   *their*   *almost*

(mohN frehr)   *(kee-lee-ah-veh too-zjoor)*   *(bo-koo dmohNd)*

soir. Mon frère Robert m'a dit qu'il y avait toujours beaucoup de monde au café Internet
                          me   *that there were always*   *lots of people*

(ahN-vwah-yahN)   *(sewr-fahN)*   *(wehb)*   *(ew-tee-lee-zahN luh treht-mahN duh tehxt)*

envoyant des emails, surfant sur le Web, et utilisant le traitement de texte.
sending   *word processor*

(suh-pahN-dahN)   *(tah-pay)*   *(klah-vyay)*

Cependant, Robert n'a pas réussi à taper très vite, parce que le clavier est différent.
however   *to type*   *keyboard*

(rahN-vehr-say)

Un soir, il a renversé du café sur la souris et sur le clavier. Le propriétaire n'était pas du
      spilled   *owner*   *wasn't at all*

tout content. Quelle horreur!

(ahN-soh-lehy)   (loo-ay)

Ensuite, le samedi, par un matin ensoleillé, Robert a loué une voiture pour aller à la
                                      rented

(kah-pah-nyuh fehr uhN pee-kneek o bohr)   (ree-vyehr mah-luh-ruhz-mahN)

campagne faire un pique–nique au bord de la rivière. Malheureusement, sa
country   *edge*   *unfortunately*

(tohN-bay ahN pahn)   (loto-root)

voiture est tombée en panne sur l'autoroute. Quelle horreur!
       broke down   *highway*

(vay-lo)   (grahN pahrk)   (plew)

Le dimanche, il a loué un vélo pour aller dans un grand parc. Il a plu presque tout le
            bicycle   *it rained*

(pnuh)   (day-gohN-flay)   (shuh-maN) (ruh-toor)

temps et son pneu s'était dégonflé sur le chemin du retour.
        got a flat tire   *road*   *return*

Quelle horreur!

(povr)   (mehm)

Pauvre Robert! Cependant, même quand
poor   *even*

il n'a pas de chance, mon
he's not lucky

(ohp-tee-meest)

frère est optimiste et dit

toujours "C'est la vie!"

DO YOU UNDERSTAND?

_____ 1. "Mieux vaut tard que jamais!"   a) la souris et le clavier

_____ 2. le patron n'a pas reçu   b) café Internet

_____ 3. est tombée en panne sur l'autoroute   c) au rendez-vous

_____ 4. a renversé du café sur   d) l'ordinateur portable

_____ 5. le pneu s'était dégonflé   e) la voiture

_____ 6. il a envoyé ses emails du   f) le vélo

_____ 7. était volé   g) un fax

MATCHING

See if you can match the past tense verb with the meaning. Look back at the story for help.

1. trouvé   _____   a) rented

2. loué   _____   b) stolen

3. perdu   _____   c) tried

4. compris   _____   d) found

5. reçu   _____   e) lost

6. arrivé   _____   f) understood

7. volé   _____   g) arrived

8. renversé   _____   h) received

9. essayé   _____   i) spilled

FOCUS

If you are involved in any kind of accident or are the victim of a theft or an attack, you need some language to help you communicate. Try to get help from **_un agent de police (ah-zhahN duh po-lees)_** or **_un gendarme (zhahN-dahrm)_**– both are words for police officer. Emergency phone numbers are usually listed on the first page of the telephone directory (just like in the U.S.). Always fill out a report and get a hold of the American consulate if you need help: **_Je dois contacter le consultat (zhuh dwah kohN-tahk-tay luh kohN-sew-lah)_** – I have to contact the consulate.

(ewr-zhahNs)
urgence
emergency

(ah lehd)
A l'aide!
Help!

(voh-luhr)
Voleur!
Thief!

(poh-lees)
Police!
Police!

(keh-skee seh pah-say)
Qu'est–ce qui s'est passé?
What happened?

(ohN mah voh-lay)
On m'a volé
They stole my…

(zhuh vuh seen-ya-lay)
Je veux signaler
I want to report

(ah-puh-lay lay pohN-pyeh)
Appelez les pompiers!
Call the fire department!

FOCUS

Find these 4 emergency words in the puzzle: *feu, police, urgence, voleur.* Then circle them.

r	v	f	d	a	x	a	w	u	g
g	w	o	e	l	f	e	k	r	o
i	t	b	l	u	s	z	o	g	w
v	f	x	s	e	u	q	l	e	t
s	u	s	j	y	u	q	i	n	t
q	i	z	x	t	w	r	g	c	i
d	p	o	l	i	c	e	u	e	g

Be sure to use the accompanying "phrase" stickers to practice what you've learned. Place them around your work and home. Build on the foundation this book provides by immersing yourself in French as much as you can. French radio and television programs may be available in your area. French films are another enjoyable way to hear the language. Read anything you can find in French, including children's books, easy novels, comics, magazines, newspapers, and even the labels on household products. Search the Internet for French websites that will give you countless opportunities to read and listen to French.

ANSWER KEY

CHAPTER 1

Practice *p.8*

1. Où <u>veux</u>-tu prendre <u>le dîner</u>?
2. Où veux-tu <u>prendre le déjeuner</u>?
3. <u>Où</u> veux-tu prendre <u>le petit déjeuner?</u>
4. <u>Où</u> veux-tu aller?

Matching *p.9*

1. E   2. A   3. D   4. B   5. C   6. F

CHAPTER 2

Number Practice *p.13*

1. quatre   2. dix   3. cinq   4. trois
5. un   6. sept   7. huit   8. neuf

Practice *p.15*

1. Anne et son amie mangent dans <u>un café.</u>
2. Julie a <u>deux</u> sandwichs.
3. Jacques <u>entre</u> dans le cafe.
4. Jacques <u>est très content</u>.

CHAPTER 3

Practice *p.19*

1. Quel âge as-tu?   2. D'où venez-vous?
3. Comment vous appelez-vous?   4. Vous êtes américain?

Practice – Asking Questions in French *p.20*

1. Est-ce que vous êtes français?   2. Tu as faim?
3. Est-ce que vous avez faim?   4. D'où venez-vous?
5. Mangez-vous les escargots?   6. Vous avez quel âge?

CHAPTER 4

Do You Understand? *p.25*

1. Isabelle   2. Il parle un peu français. (He speaks a little french.)

3. deux éclairs au chocolat (two chocolate eclairs)   4. Isabelle
5. dans une boulangerie (in a bakery)

Practice: What would you like? *p.27*

1. onze   2. dix-huit   3. quinze
4. trois   5. cinq   6. deux

CHAPTER 5

Practice *p.31*

1. house(maison)   2. years old (ans)   3. nice (sympathique)
4. funny (marrante) 5. work/job (travail) 6. train (train)   7. car (voiture)

Crossword Puzzle: Colors *p.32*

Across: 3. rouge 6. gris 7. marron 8. vert
Down: 1. jaune 2. bleu 3. rose 4. orange 5. blanc

Practice: Days of the Week *p.33*

3 mercredi   7 dimanche   2 mardi   5 vendredi   1 lundi   6 samedi   4 jeudi

CHAPTER 6

Practice: Ordinal Number *p.37*

A is premier   F is sixième
B is deuxième   G is septième
C is troisième   H is huitième
D is quatrième   I is neuvième
E is cinquième   J is dixième

Practice: Comprenez-vous? *p.39*

1. non   2. oui   3. non   4. non

CHAPTER 7

Practice: Translating picture captions *p.42*

1. The mother is at the beach during the summer.
2. The father is in the mountains during the winter.
3. The brother is hiking during the autumn.
4. The sisters are looking at the flowers in the spring.

Practice: Translating story sentences *p.44*

A. French to English

1. My father prefers winter.
2. My brother, Robert, who is 17, likes to hike in the forest.
3. When do we take our vacation?
4. From time to time, we also hike in the winter and spring.

B. English to French

1. J'ai vingt (20) ans.
2. Il aime les couleurs de l'automne (orange, rouge, jaune, marron).
3. Moi aussi! Janine et moi aimons les belles fleurs.
4. En juin, juillet et août nous allons souvent à la plage.

Focus: Definite Articles – Noun Gender Practice *p.45*

1. la soeur	2. la plage	3. la famille	4. le fromage
5. la voiture	6. l'homme	7. le matin	8. la saison
9. le musée	10. la rue		

CHAPTER 8

Practice: Family Members *p.49*

1. a) Patrick b) le frère   2. a) Morgane b) la belle-soeur   3. a) René b) le père

4. a) Sophie b) la mère   5. a) Andrée b) la femme

6. a) Hélène b) la belle-mère   7. a) Albert b) le beau-père   8. a) Nathalie b) la fille

Questions: *p.50*   1. Andrée   2. Sophie   3. Patrick   4. Nathalie   5. Pierre

Focus: Adjectives *p.50*

1. la grande femme	2. la petite fille	3. le beau mari
4. la belle grand-mère	5. la nièce intelligente	6. les pères intelligents

Practice: Possessive Adjectives *p.51*

1. ma	2. ma	3. son	4. ta	5. leurs
6. votre	7. mes	8. leur	9. sa	10. nos

CHAPTER 9

Practice: Comprenez-vous? *p.55*

1. Elise
2. en Alaska
3. à Paris
4. tous les jours sauf le dimanche (du lundi au samedi)

Matching *p.55*

Elise (la fille)	Maman
2, 3, 5, 7, 8	1, 4, 6

Practice – Quel temps fait-il? *p.56*

1. il fait chaud	2. il pleut beaucoup	3. il fait mauvais	4. il neige
5. il y a du vent	6. il fait humide	7. il fait beau	

Practice and Review *p.57*

1. neige   2. froid   3. beaucoup   4. ici   5. printemps

CHAPTER 10

Do You Understand? *p.61*

1. F   2. T   3. F   4. F   5. T

Practice: Time *p.62*

1. d   2. e   3. a   4. c   5. b

CHAPTER 11

Do You Understand? *p.68*

1. D   2. C   3. E   4. B   5. A

Practice: Prepositions *p.69*

1. dans   2. sur   3. sur   4. derrière   5. sous   6. à côté

Write Two Sentences

Possible answers:
1. Il y a un livre sur le tapis.   2. Le chien est à côté du lit.
3. Le chien est sur le tapis.   4. Le livre est par terre.
5. Les jouets sont par terre.

CHAPTER 12

Matching *p.72*

1. c   2. a   3. b   4. e   5. f   6. d

Practice: Passé composé *p.74*

1. ai téléphoné   2. avons parlé   3. a joué
4. a regardé   5. avons nagé   6. sommes allés

CHAPTER 13

Practice: Food Vocabulary Crossword *p.80*

Across: 3. gâteau 5. vin 7. fromage 8. poisson
Down: 1. champignon 2. jambon 4. glace 6. lait 7. fraise

Review: Vrai ou faux *p.81*

1. vrai–T   2. vrai –T   3. faux–F (vin blanc)   4. faux–F (saumon)
5. faux–F (glace à la vanille)

CHAPTER 14

Oui ou non? *p.85*

1. oui   2. oui   3. non (chez Christine)   4. non (40th)   5. oui

Practice: Qu'est–ce que vous avez? *p.87*

1. c   2. f   3. g   4. a   5. h   6. b   7. e   8. d

CHAPTER 15

Do You Understand? *p.92*

1. F   2. T   3. F   4. T

Word Scramble: Clothing *p.93*

PEUJ = jupe   EOBR = robe   TANALOPN = pantalon
ECHIISEMER = chemisier   LAFDURO = foulard

Elle	met	une	robe	rouge
1 2 3 4	5 6 7	8 9 10	11 12 13 10	14 15 16 1

CHAPTER 16

Do You Understand? *p.98*

1. c   2. g   3. e   4. a   5. f   6. b   7. d

Matching: Verbs *p.98*

1. d   2. a   3. e   4. f   5. h   6. g   7. b   8. i   9. c

GLOSSARY

The numbers after each entry indicate the chapter where the word first occurs
or where there is more detailed information about that word.

m = masculine
f = feminine
pl = plural

FRENCH WORD	ENGLISH	CHAPTER
à	to, in, at	1
à côté de	next to	6
a votre santé	cheers	14
acheter	to buy	15
adorer	to adore, love	11
âge(m)	age	3
aider	to help	15
aimer	to like, love	5,11
aller	to go	1
alors	then	1
américain(m),américaine(f)	American	7
ami(m), amie(f)	friend	1
amusant(m),amusante (f)	amusing	12
ananas(m)	pineapple	13
anglais(m)	English	7
année(f)	year	7
anniversaire(m)	birthday	14
ans(m)	years	3
août(m)	August	7
après	after	9
après-midi(m)	afternoon	10
arriver	to arrive	10
artiste(m,f)	artist	2
assez	enough, quite	11
attendre	to wait for	5
au contraire	on the contrary	3
au revoir	goodbye	4
aujourd' hui	today	6
aussi	also	7
automne(m)	autumn	7
autre	other	7
avec	with	5
avion(m)	airplane	7
avis(m)	opinion	7
avoir	to have	3
avoir besoin de	to have need of	8
avoir raison	to be right	15
avril(m)	April	7
banque(f)	bank	6
beau(m),belle(f),beaux(pl)	beautiful	6
beaucoup	a lot	1
beau-père(m)	father-in-law	8
belle-mère(f)	mother-in-law	8
belle-soeur(f)	sister-in-law	8
bien	good, well	1
bien sûr	sure, of course	3
bière(f)	beer	13
billet(m)	ticket	4
blaguer	to joke	12
blanc(m), blanche(f)	white	5
bleu(m), bleue(f)	blue	5
boire	to drink	13
boisson(f)	drink(noun)	13
bon(m), bonne(f)	good	1
bonjour	hello,good morning	1
boulangerie (f)	bakery	4
boulevard(m)	boulevard	6
boum(f)	party	12
bouteille(f)	bottle	4
bras(m)	arm	14
bureau(m)	office, desk	16
c'est	it is	1
ça (cela)	it	1
café	coffee	4
café(m)	café	2
campagne(m)	countryside	4
cartes(f)	(playing) cards	11
carte postale(f)	postcard	4
ce(m), cette(f), ces(pl)	this	15
cependant	however	7
chaise(f)	chair	11
chambre(f)	bedroom	11

FRENCH WORD	ENGLISH	CHAPTER
champignon(m)	mushroom	13
chance(f)	luck	2
chapeau(m)	hat	8
chaque	each, every	5
chance(f)	luck	16
chat(m), chatte(f)	cat	11
chaud	hot	9
chéri(m), chérie (f)	dear	9
cheveux(m)	hair	8
chez	at (a place)	14
chien(m)	dog	6
chocolat(m)	chocolate	4
choisir	to choose	5
cinéma	cinema (movie theater)	6
cinq	five	2
cinquième	fifth	6
combien	how much	4
commencer	to begin	14
comment	how, what (did you say?)	3,10
comprendre	to understand	4
concert(m)	concert	10
confortable	comfortable	11
content(m), contente(f)	happy	2
copain(m), copine(f)	friend	13
corbeille à papier(f)	wastebasket	12
corps(m)	body	14
couleur(f)	color	7
course(f)	race	6
court(m), courte(f)	short	8
coûter	to cost	4
cravate(f)	necktie	7
cuisine(f)	kitchen	11
cuisiner	to cook	11
d'abord	at first	16
d'accord	OK, agreed	2
d'ailleurs	besides	12
dans	in	1
de l'autre côté de	on the other side of	6
de rien, je vous en prie	you're welcome	2
de, d'	from, to, of	4
décembre(m)	December	3
dedans	inside	11
dehors	outside	11
déjà	already	7
déjeuner(m)	lunch	1
demain	tomorrow	9
demander	to ask	1
demi(m), demie(f)	half	2
depuis	since	14
derrière	behind	10
des	some,	11
descendre	to go down	7
désirer	to desire, want	6,10
désolé	sorry	13
deux	two	4
deuxième	second	2
devant	in front of	11
devoir	to have to, must	6
dimanche(m)	Sunday	5
dîner(m)	dinner, to dine	16
dire	to say, tell	10
dix	ten	1
dix-huit	eighteen	2
dixième	tenth	4
dix-neuf	nineteen	6
dix-sept	seventeen	4
docteur(m)	doctor	4
doigt(m)	finger	14
donc	so	2
donner	to give	2
dormir	to sleep	11
douze	twelve	1
droit(m), droite(f)	right	4
dynamique	dynamic	6
eau minérale(f)	mineral water	7
elle	she, it	1
elles(f)	they	1
en	in, some	1
en avance	early	2
en bas	downstairs	10
en face de	facing	11

FRENCH WORD	ENGLISH	CHAPTER
en fait	in fact	6
en haut	upstairs	11
en retard	late	10
en train de	in the middle of doing something	2
encore	still	12
enfant(m)	child	8
ennuyeux(m), ennuyeuse(f)	boring	5
ensemble	together	5
ensuite	then, next	5
entrée(f)	first course	13
entrer	to enter	6
envoyer	to send	16
escargot(m)	snail	13
essayer	to try on	15
et	and	3
état(m)	state	3
été	summer	7
étoile(f)	star	5
étonnant	astonishing, surprising	10
être	to be	3
euro(m)	monetary unit of Europe	4
faim(m)	hunger	2
faire	to do	9
faire des courses	to go shopping	6
famille(f)	family	6
fatigué	tired	7
femme(f)	woman, wife	3,8
femme d'affaires(f)	businesswoman	8
fenêtre(f)	window	11
fermé	closed	6
fêter	celebrate	14
feu(m)	fire	16
février(m)	February	7
fille(f)	girl, daughter	3,8
fils(m)	son	8
finir	to finish	5
fleur(f)	flower	5
foot, football(m)	soccer	11
forêt(f)	forest	5
four(m)	oven	11
fraise(f)	strawberry	13
français(m)	French	7
frère(m)	brother	7
froid	cold	7
fromage(m)	cheese	13
gagner	to win	6
garçon(m)	boy	2
gare(f)	train station	10
gâteau(m)	cake	1
gauche	left	6
gendarme(m)	policeman	16
génial	great	6
gens(m)	people	14
glace(f)	ice cream	13
gorge(f)	throat	14
grand(m), grande(f)	big, tall	6
grand-père(m)	grandfather	5
grave	serious	8
gris	gray	3
habiter	to live	5
heure(f)	hour	10
hier	yesterday	9
hiver(m)	winter	7
homme(m)	man	1
hôtel(m)	hotel	5
huit	eight	2
huitième	eighth	6
humide	humid	1
ici	here	7
il	he, it	1
ils	they	1
il y a	there is, there are	7, 10
immédiatement	immediately	6
intelligent(m), intelligente(f)	intelligent	8
intéressant(m), intéressante(f)	interesting	5
jamais	never	15,16
jambon	ham	13
janvier(m)	January	7
jardin(m)	garden	5
jaune	yellow	5
je	I	13
jeudi(m)	Thursday	3

FRENCH WORD	ENGLISH	CHAPTER
joli(m), jolie(f)	pretty	15
jouer	to play	5
juillet(m)	July	7
juin(m)	June	7
jupe(f)	skirt	15
jusqu'à	until	6
l',le(m), la(f), les(pl)	the	3
là-bas	over there	15
lait (m)	milk	13
lentement	slowly	4
leur,leurs	their	8
libre	free	11
lit(m)	bed	1
livre(m)	book	11
loin	far	7
long(m), longue(f)	long	8
louer	to rent	16
loup(m)	wolf	13
lui	him	2
lundi(m)	Monday	5
lunettes(f pl)	glasses	8
madame(f)	Mrs.,madam	10
mademoiselle(f)	miss	10
magasin(m)	store	6
mai(m)	May	7
main(f)	hand	14
maintenant	now	10
mais	but	7
maison(f)	house	3
malade	sick	14
maman (f)	Mom, Mama	9
manger	to eat	1
manteau(m)	coat	15
maquillage (m)	make-up (comestics)	7
marcher	to walk	5
mardi(m)	Tuesday	5
mari(m)	husband	8
marié	married	8
marrant(m), marrante(f)	funny,humorous	5
marron	brown	7
mars(m)	March	7
matin(m)	morning	1
mauvais(m), mauvaise(f)	bad	9
même	same	15
merci	thank you	4
mercredi(m)	Wednesday	5
mère(f)	mother	7
mettre	to put(on)	15
midi(m)	noon	10
mieux	better	2,7
minuit(m)	midnight	10
moi	me	7
moins	less, minus	10
mois(m)	month	7
mon(m), ma(f), mes(pl)	my	8
monde(m)	world	7
monsieur(m)	sir	13
montagne(f)	mountain	7
monter	to go up	6
mot	word	7
musée d'art(m)	art museum	6
n'est-ce pas?	isn't it?, aren't you, etc	10
nager	to swim	13
ne...pas	not	10
neige (f)	snow	9
neuf	nine	2
neuvième	ninth	6
neveu(m)	nephew	8
nez(m)	nose	14
nièce(f)	niece	8
noir(m), noire(f)	black	5
nombre(m)	number	13
non	no	2
notre(f,m), nos	our	7
nous	we	1
nouveau(m), nouvelle(f)	new	12
novembre(m)	November	7
occupé	busy	5
octobre(m)	October	7
on	one, we	1,5
oncle(m)	uncle	7
onze	eleven	4

FRENCH WORD	ENGLISH	CHAPTER
orange	orange(color), fruit	5,13
où	where	1
ou	or	10
oui	yes	3
ouvert(m), ouverte(f)	open	6
ordinateur(m)	computer	11,16
pain(m)	bread	4
pantalon(m)	pants	15
par	by	16
par terre	on the ground	11
parce que	because	12
parler	to speak	1
partir	to leave	15
pâtes(f pl)	pasta	1
pauvre	poor	9
pendant	during	9
penser	to think	12
perdre	to lose	11
père(m)	father	5
personne(f)	person	11
petit déjeuner(m)	breakfast	1
petit(m),petite(f)	small	8
petite-fille(f)	granddaughter	8
petit-fils(m)	grandson	8
peu	little	12
peur	fear	14
peut-être	perhaps, maybe	7
pied(m)	foot	14
plage(f)	beach	1
pleuvoir	to rain	9
plus	more	6
pneu(m)	tire	16
poids(m)	weight	14
pomme(f)	apple	13
pont(m)	bridge	6
portable(m)	cellular phone	16
porter	to wear	15
poulet(m)	chicken	13
pour	in order to,for	6
pourquoi	why	13
pouvoir	to be able to	7
préférer	to prefer	6
premier(m), première(f)	first	1
prendre	to take	6
près de	near	2
présenter	to introduce	7
presque	almost	11
prêt	ready	15
printemps(m)	spring	7
prochain	next	9
professeur(m)	teacher	2
programmeur(m)	computer programmer	5
quai(m)	platform	10
quand	when	7
quatorze	fourteen	4
quatre	four	2
quatrième	fourth	6
que	that, what, which	10
quel(m), quelle(f)	what,which	7
quelque chose	something	13
qu'est-ce que	what	4
qui	who	9
quinze	fifteen	4
randonner	to hike	7
regarder	to look at	2
rendez-vous(m)	arrangement to meet	16
rendre visite à	to visit (someone)	9
renverser	to spill	16
répondre	to respond	7
rester	to stay	2
réunion(f)	meeting	15
robe(f)	dress	5
rose	pink	5
rouge	red	6
rue(f)	street	7
rhume(m)	cold (noun)	14
saison(f)	season	7
salle(f)	room	11
salut	hi	14
samedi(m)	Saturday	5
santé(f)	health	3
s'appeler	to be called	9

FRENCH WORD	ENGLISH	CHAPTER
s'asseoir	to sit down	11
sauf	except	14
saumon(m)	salmon	13
se promener	to go for a walk	6
se sentir	to feel	14
seize	sixteen	4
semaine(f)	week	5
sens(m)	meaning	14
sentir	to smell	11
sept	seven	2
septembre(m)	September	7
septième	seventh	6
s'il vous plaît, s'il te plaît	please	2
six	six	2
sixième	sixth	6
skier	to ski	7
soeur(f)	sister	8
soie(f)	silk	15
soif(f)	thirst	3
soir(m)	evening	10
soleil(m)	sunny	9
son(m), sa(f), ses(pl)	his, her	8
sortir	to leave, go out	2
sous	under	11
souvent	often	7
stylo(m)	pen	4
sur	on	11
surtout	especially	7
sympathique, sympa	nice	5
ton(m), ta(f), tes(pl)	your (familiar)	11
taille(f)	size	15
tant pis	nevermind	6
tante (f)	aunt	8
tapis(m)	rug, carpet	11
tarte(f)	pie	13
temps(m)	time, weather	9,10
tête(f)	head	14
thé	tea	13
timbre(f)	stamp	4
toujours	always	16
tourner	to turn	6
tous les deux	both	5
tout droit	straight ahead	6
tout le monde	everyone	7
tout(m), toute(f), tous(pl)	all	1
train(m)	train	5
travail(m)	work,job	6,9
travailler	to work	9
traverser	to cross	6
treize	thirteen	4
très	very	2
triste	sad	2
trois	three	2
troisième	third	6
trop	too	1
tu	you (informal)	7
un(m), une(f)	a, one	7
vacances(f pl)	vacation	7
valise(f)	suitcase	2
vélo(m)	bicycle	16
vendeur(m), vendeuse(f)	salesman, saleswoman	4
vendre	to sell	5
vendredi(m)	Friday	5
venir	to come	9
vent(m)	wind	9
ventre(m)	stomach	14
verre(m)	glass	10
vert	green	5
vêtements(m pl)	clothing	15
viande(f)	meat	1
vie(f)	life	16
vieux(m), vieille(f)	old	11
vin(m)	wine	13
vingt	twenty	3
visiter	to visit(a place)	6
voici	here is, here are	3
voilà	there is, there are	4
voir	to see	12
voiture(f)	car	1
voler	to steal, to fly	16
voleur(m)	thief	16
votre(m,f) vos (pl)	your	8

FRENCH WORD	ENGLISH	CHAPTER
voudrais	would like	1
vouloir	to want, wish	7
vous	you (formal)	3
voyage(m)	trip	7
voyager	to travel	7
vrai	true	6
vraiment	really	12
yeux(m pl)	eyes	5
zut	darn	10

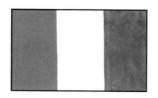

FRANCE

France, the largest country in western Europe, and the world's top tourist destination, has a long and a rich history with the United States:

- The Founding Fathers of the U.S. were all disciples of French philosophers like Montesquieu, Diderot, and Voltaire. Beginning in the early nineteenth century, an astonishingly large number of Americans (writers in particular) have found inspiration and acceptance in Paris by making it their temporary home. (Think Ernest Hemingway, John Steinbeck, Art Buchwald, Gertrude Stein, Janet Flanner, Henry James, Irwin Shaw, James Baldwin, W.H. Auden and many, many more.)

- The United States has been influenced by French architecture, food and wine, fashion, dance, film, arts, philosophy, and political thought. France embraces American culture through movies, music, books, TV and "franglais" (like *le parking, le fast food, le shopping, le marketing, le rock,* and *cool,* to name a few).

- The U.S. and France were allies during the War of 1812, the U.S. Civil War, and during both World Wars where fighting on French soil killed over a million French soldiers. To honor the friendship that was established between the two countries during the American Revolution, France presented the Statue of Liberty to the United States in 1886. It remains a symbol of not only freedom and democracy, but a reminder of the long-term friendship between the U.S. and France.

- Slightly smaller than Texas, France is amazingly diverse in its scenery and landscape. Beyond the large metropolitan areas like Paris, you will find rolling green hills, snow-capped mountains, and a sunny, Mediterranean coast. The super fast TGV trains leaving Paris make traveling around France quick and easy. Here are just a few areas you might want to visit:

1 Normandy: Mont-St- Michel; Bayeux tapestry; D-Day beaches; Camembert

2 Alsace: Strasbourg (where *pâté de foie gras* was invented); excellent food and wine; colorful festivals

3 Loire Valley: Magnificent castles (Chenonceaux, Chambord, Chinon); Vouvray wine

4 Bordeaux (region): Atlantic beaches; La Rochelle; Futuroscope (a cinema theme park); Cognac; Bordeaux wines

5 Provence: Lavender fields, fascinating cities (Arles, Avignon, Marseille), outdoor markets, superb cuisine

OTHER FRENCH SPEAKING COUNTRIES

French is spoken on five continents and is the first or second language in close to 50 countries. Some local dialects exist, but knowing your fundamental French will help you have a rewarding experience in francophone countries as you get to know the people who live there. Here are only some of the places you may be able to practice your French someday if you travel there.

BELGIUM
la Belgique

- Flemish speak Dutch; Walloons speak French; many people speak English
- Bruges– "Venice of the North" because of its canals; medieval architecture
- Known for its mussels, chocolate, beer, lace and warm hospitality

SWITZERLAND
la Suisse

- French is one of four national languages (along with German, Italian, and Romansh)
- Seventy percent of country covered by the Alps
- Frequent trains that take you through spectacular scenery run all over (even up steep inclines)
- Discover the "Swiss Riviera" along Lake Geneva: Montreaux, Vevey, Lausanne and Geneva
- Sample Swiss culinary specialties like raclette and fondue

TAHITI
le Tahiti

- One of 120 islands of the French Polynesia archipelago in the Pacific Ocean
- Tropical paradise and close to islands of Moorea, Bora Bora, and others
- Smoked breadfruit, banana groves, gorgeous flowers, waterfalls, Gaughin Museum

SENEGAL
le Sénégal

- Dakar, port city and capital, has open-air markets, outdoor cafes, many art galleries and studios
- Peaceful and beautiful Island of Gorée was once center of slave trade. Visit the preserved "Slave House"
- 350 miles of beaches – go south of Dakar for best locations
- "Pink Lake" shallow, warm, and completely pink. Everything floats on it because of its high salinity.

PARIS MONUMENTS AND MUSEUMS

The Eiffel Tower, built in 1889, is of course the most well-known of Paris monuments and one that is very impressive close up as well as far away. It is about 1,000 feet tall, contains nearly 7,000 tons of metal and has three levels, accessible by elevators or by climbing the 1,665 steps. Be sure to catch a glimpse of *la tour Eiffel (eh-fel)* at night when it is illuminated.

The Arc de Triomphe, the largest triumphal arch in the world, is a massive monument that was built by Napoleon I to commemorate his victories. Located at the western end of the famous Champs-Elysées *(shaN-zay-lee-zay)*, there are 12 avenues (the Place d'Etoile – the "star") that radiate from the arc. The bustling traffic moves in a circular pattern, which is viewable from the observation deck at the top of the arc (where you also get a panoramic view of the Champs-Elysées as well as other Paris landmarks).

Known for its gargoyles and the Hunchback, Notre Dame Cathedral *(nohtr dahm)* is a masterpiece of Gothic architecture, constructed during the 12th and 13th centuries. It is located in the center of Paris on the "Ile de la Cité", the island in the River Seine *(sehn)*. Climb to the top for a bird's eye view of the city or admire it from the river when you take a "Bateau-Mouche" tour down the Seine.

A visit to Paris would not be complete without viewing at least some of the art in the largest museum in the western world, the Louvre. One of the entrances to the Louvre is through the glass pyramid built by the American architect, I.M.Pei. To view Europe's greatest collection of Impressionist art, go to the Orsay Museum (Musée d'Orsay), across the river from the Louvre. Don't miss the Pompidou Center for a chance to see an incredible collection of modern art.

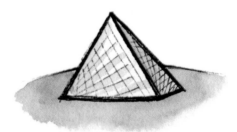

Nearly 100 museums in and around Paris allow you many exciting choices, whether your interests are fashion, wine, technology, sculpture, stamps, dolls, photography, music, or just about anything. Take advantage of special exhibits that may be open during your visit. Other places to include on your itinerary: Versailles (just outside of Paris), the grand palace of the kings, Père Lachaise Cemetery, where you can find the graves of famous French citizens as well as American rocker, Jim Morrison, and the Grande Arche de la Défense, the enormous Twentieth Century complex in the suburb of La Défense that is in sharp contrast to the historical significance of the Arc de Triomphe.

QUEBEC

Three times the size of France, Québec, *"La Belle Province"*, is Canada's largest province. About half of the population of *Québec* (kay-behk) lives in *Montréal* (mohN-ray-al), a festive city known for its night life and variety of restaurants. Most of the other "Quebecers" or *Québecois* (kay-bay-kwa) live in the other cities and towns along the St. Lawrence river, including Québec City, the provincial capital and magical city that feels like you are in Europe with its cobblestone streets and historical significance. The scenery is spectacular in Québec. There are close to a million lakes, over one hundred thousand rivers, and about half the land is forested. It is known for very cold, snowy winters, but it has four distinct seasons, and tourists visit at all times of year.

French is the official language of Québec. *Québécois* is the name of the language as well as the people. The vast majority of the people are *francophones* (French speaking). In fact, Montréal has more French speakers than any other city in the world besides Paris. Many of the 10% who call themselves "anglophones" are also bilingual. Most of the anglophones live in the Montreal area so you will hear English spoken there (and to a lesser extent in Québec City), but you will not find English on road signs, maps, or brochures. It helps to become familiar with *Québécois*. It will sound different from "France" French not only in the differences in pronunciation, but in the many unique words and expressions. Here is a partial list of words and expressions that will help you:

Québécois	French	English
la fin de semaine	le week-end	weekend
arrêt	le stop	stop
le stationnement	le parking	parking
magasiner	shopper	to shop
le déjeuner	le petit déjeuner	breakfast
le dîner	le déjeuner	lunch
le souper	le dîner	dinner
un dépanneur	un petit magasin	a convenience store
une broue	une bière	a beer
une patate frite	des frites	French fries
une tabagie	un tabac	cigarette stand
courriel	email	email
un char	une voiture	a car
mon chum	mon ami, mon copain	my friend/buddy
une vue	un film	a movie
des flots	des enfants	children
des barniques	des lunettes	eyeglasses
un pitou	un chien	a dog
un minou	un chat	a cat
il fait frette	il fait très froid	it's very cold
il mouille	il pleut	it's raining
sacrer son camp	partir/quitter	to leave
Pantoute!	Pas du tout!	Not at all!

2

1

4

3

6

5

8

7

(sah meh tay-gahl)
Ça m'est égal.
It's all the same to me.

1

(ohN nyee-vah)
On y va!
Let's Go!

2

(unuhm)
un homme
man

3

(boN-zhoor)
Bonjour.
Good morning

4

(ewn fahm)
une femme
woman

5

(mahN-zhay)
manger
to eat

6

(luh puh-tee day-zhuh-nay)
le petit déjeuner
breakfast

7

(zhay faN)
J'ai faim!
I'm Hungry!

8

10

12

14

16

9

11

13

15

(kohN-tahN)
content
happy

9

(treest)
triste
sad

10

(ah-mee)
amie
female friend

11

(fro-mahzh)
fromage
cheese

12

(dun)
donne
give

13

(zhay swahf)
J'ai soif.
I'm thirsty.

14

(zhuh swee fah-tee-gay)
Je suis fatigue.
I'm tired.

15

(suh neh pah grahv)
Ce n'est pas grave
*Don't worry about it/ that's okay/
It's not that serious*

16

18

17

20

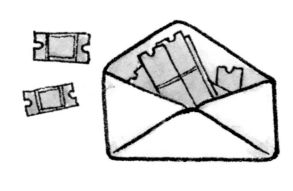

19

22

21

24

23

(kahrt po-stahl)
cartes postales
postcards

17

(taNbr)
timbres
stamps

18

(bee-yeh)
billets
tickets

19

(kah-fay)
cafés
coffee

20

(stee-lo)
stylos
pens

21

(ahN-new-yuh/ahN-new-yuhz)
ennuyeux/ennuyeuse
boring

22

(ah-vwahr luh sahN sho)
avoir le sang chaud
to be quick tempered

23

(lah meh-zohN)
le maison
house

24

26

25

28

27

30

29

32

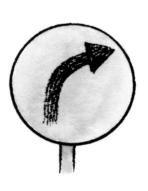

31

(lah vwa-tewr)
la voiture
car

25

(lay-twahl)
l'étoile
star

26

(duh lotre ko-tay duh)
de l'autre côté de
on the other side

27

(ahN fahs duh)
en face de
facing

28

(ah gohsh)
à gauche
to the left

29

(too drwah)
tout droit
straight ahead

30

(ah drwaht)
à droite
to the right

31

(luh shah-po)
le chapeau
hat

32

34

33

36

35

38

37

40

39

(luh mah-ree)
le mari
husband

(lah fahm)
la femme
wife

33

(eel feh dew vahN)
Il fait du vent.
It's windy.

34

(eel pluh)
Il pleut.
It's raining.

35

(eel feh dew soh-lay)
Il fait du soleil.
It's sunny.

36

(eel nehzh)
Il neige.
It's snowing.

37

(eh-trahN nah-vahNs)
être en avance
to be early

38

(eh-trahN ruh-tahr)
être en retard
to be late

39

(prohpr koh muhN soo nuhf)
Propre comme un sou neuf.
Neat as a pin.

40

42

41

44

43

46

45

48

47

(ahN-o)
En haut
upstairs

41

(lohr-dee-nah-tuhr)
l'ordinateur (m)
computer

42

(lay frew-ee)
les fruits (m)
fruit

43

(keh-skuh) (voo voo-lay mahN-zhay)
Qu'est-ce que vous voulez manger?
What do you want to eat?

44

(zhuh muh sahN mahl)
Je me sens mal.
I feel sick.

45

(luh tay-lay-fohn pohr-tahbl)
(le téléphone) portable
cell phone

46

(tohN-bay ahN pahn)
tombée en panne
broke down

47

(ah-puh-lay lay pohN-pyeh)
Appelez les pompiers!
Call the fire department!

48

(ohN nyee-vah)
On y va!
Let's go!

(BoN-zhoor)
Bonjour.
Good morning.

(sah-vah)
Ça Va?
How are you?

(luh deenay)
le dîner
dinner

(zhay faN)
J'ai faim!
I'm hungry!

Ehk-skew-zay-mwah
Excusez-moi!
Excuse me! Sorry!

(KohN-mahN voo zah-play voo)
Comment vous appelez-vous?
What's you name?

(Ehs Kuh voo zeht fah-tee-gay)
Est ce que vous êtes fatigué?
Are you tired?

(Mehr-see byaN) (bo Koo)
Merci bien *or* merci beaucoup.
Thank you very much.

(O ruh vwahr)
Au revoir!
Good bye!

Comprenez-vous?
Do you understand?

(Kehl than feh-teel)
Quel temps fait-il?
What's the weather?

(Eel feh frwah)
Il fait froid.
It's cold

(voo-za-vay luhr, seel-voo-pleh)
Vous avez l'heure, s'il vous plaît?
Do you have the time, please?

(Pwee-zhuh voo zay day)
Puis-je vous aider?
Can I help you?

(dah-fehr)
voyage d'affaires
business trip

(sah meh tay-gahl)
Ça m'est égal.
It's all the same to me.

(ewn fahm)
une femme
woman

(vuh)
veux
want

(Zhuh prahN luh traN)
Je prends le train.
I'm taking the train.

(kohN-tahN)
content
happy

(doo vuh-nay voo)
D'où venez-vous?
Where do you come from?

(Keh lahzh ah tew)
Quel âge as-tu?
How old are you?

(Zhay buh-zwaN duh)
J'ai besoin de…
I need…

(NohN mehr-see)
Non, merci.
No thank you.

(Leh pohN)
le pont
bridge

(Vwah-see mah fah-mee-y)
Voici ma famille.
This is my family.

(Eel feh sho)
Il fait chaud.
It's hot.

(Lah suh mehn dehr-nyehr)
la semaine dernière.
last week

(kens kuh tew vuh mahn-zhay)
Qu'est-ce que tu veux manger?
What do you want to eat?

(Myuh vo tahr kuh zhah-meh)
Mieux vaut tard que jamais!
Better late than never!

(Lah ay ro pohr)
l'aéroport
airport